What Angry Kids Need

*Parenting Your Angry Child
Without Going Mad*

by
Jennifer Anne Brown, MSW
and Pam Provonsha Hopkins, MSW

Illustrated by
Mits Katayama

Parenting Press
Seattle, Washington

Printed in the United States of America
Designed by Margarite Hargrave Design
Illustrated by Mits Katayama

ISBN 1-884734-84-7 or 978-1-884734-84-7, paperback
ISBN 1-884734-85-5 or 978-1-884734-85-4, library binding

Library of Congress Cataloging-in-Publication Data
Brown, Jennifer Anne, 1974-
  What angry kids need : parenting your angry child without
        going mad / by Jennifer Anne Brown and Pam Provonsha
        Hopkins.
     p. cm.
  Includes bibliographical references and index.
  ISBN 978-1-884734-84-7
  1. Parenting. 2. Parent and child. 3. Emotional problems of
        children. I. Hopkins, Pam Provonsha, 1959- II. Title.
  HQ755.8.B76 2008
  649'.154--dc22
                                2007051106

Parenting Press
P.O. Box 75267
Seattle, Washington 98175

*To see all our helpful publications and services for parents,
caregivers, and children, go to www.ParentingPress.com.*

Dedication

To Jacob, who gives me reasons to laugh every day,

To Chris, whose playfulness and warmth always remind me to make time for fun.

—Jennifer

To Jessie, whose creativity, perseverance, and courage inspire me,

To Trevor, whose empathy, loyalty, and sense of humor warm me,

To Terry, who supports me, makes me laugh, and continues to surprise me.

—Pam

To our parents, who parented by heart and good sense, without benefit of parenting books,

And to all the members of the Attach Team over the years—staff, parents, and children—for your wisdom, creativity, and inspiration.

—Pam and Jennifer

Contents

Introduction   6

1: Understanding Anger   9

2: What Makes Kids Angry?   16

3: Dealing with Feelings   27

4: Tools Kids Need to Manage Intense
   Feelings   42

5: Tools Kids Need to Solve Individual and
   Social Problems   61

6: Tools Kids Need to Deal with Problems
   Outside Their Control   74

7: Tools Parents Need to Take Care of Their
   Own Intense Feelings   87

8: Help! Nothing Is Working   101

Appendices

A. The Face of Anger at Each Developmental
   Stage   110

B. Factors that May Affect Attachment   120

C. Practical Questions About Time-Out   121

D. Getting Started with Conflict Management   124

E. Steps to Implement a Reinforcement System   128

F. Co-Parenting Agreement   130

G. How Skillfully Do You Manage Anger?
   Worksheet   132

Recommended Reading   *134*

Index   *137*

Introduction

Do you have a child in your life who is struggling? Does your child scream his head off when you tell him "no," kick his sister in the shins because she looked at him wrong, or slam the door and yell, "I hate you" because you suggested a bedroom clean-up might be in order? If you recognize your child in these examples, you already know how frustrating it is to parent kids like this. In fact, you may wonder sometimes who is angrier, you or your child!

Kids who yell, kick, hit, throw chairs, grab toys, or attack others are expressing their feelings, however confused and misguided their actions might be in the moment. The good news is there are things you can do every day to make life go more smoothly with your expressive child. *What Angry Kids Need* will help you understand your child's anger, and it will provide tools for you and your child to manage intense feelings.

What Angry Kids Need is for you if your child is between one and twelve years of age and:
- rarely expresses anger, but instead holds it in
- has occasional tantrums or meltdowns
- seems more intense, dramatic, or emotional than other children
- is angry, explosive, and sometimes hurts you or others
- has health or developmental issues that make it hard to manage intense feelings
- has experienced trauma or loss and is out of control

Anger is a normal part of life. Its expressions take many forms, some visible, others less so. *Healthy communication* of all feelings, and especially anger, is a cornerstone of development. It helps children grow into well-adjusted people with meaningful connections to others. Our experience as parents and professionals shows us that with the right tools and support, kids' daily snits and even intense angry outbursts can be opportunities to build relationships and foster growth.

• • •

We have many years of experience working in treatment programs for children who struggle with intense emotions and extreme behavior. As professionals working with these children, we find them immensely rewarding because they have the energy and passion to get their needs met, if given the right tools. In fact, we really like these kids! We have seen the wonderful results when children, even very young ones, are given the support and skills they need to express feelings in healthy ways.

The examples we use throughout this book come from our own childhoods, our own children, and the children and parents we have worked with over the years. You may initially feel that some of the examples are unrealistic, or too smooth and orderly. However, don't be too quick to assume that you can't achieve similar outcomes. Whether you experience success after the first, the fiftieth, or the eighty-fifth time you use the skills we suggest will depend on various factors; however, over time the skills are effective. (They probably worked the second time on Pam, a cooperative middle child, and perhaps the one hundred forty-second time on Jennifer, an energetic spitfire likely to throw a tantrum!)

We hope you will keep this book close at hand for ready reference, perhaps on the kitchen counter next to the coffee maker or on the bedside table for a few minutes' reading before you drop from exhaustion, worn out by your angry child. Use this book in the way that is most helpful to you. The first two chapters lay the foundation for understanding anger; subsequent chapters get right into the skills you need to manage your kid's behavior. If you are overwhelmed *right now*, go directly to the chapter that offers you immediate practical help. You can always come back to the first two chapters when your child has calmed down.

Here is the most important message we hope you take away from this book: What angry kids really need are supportive adults who can help them understand and manage intense emotions. Using these skills over time will make a big difference in the day-to-day life of your child and family. In the long run, you will be helping your young child grow into a healthy person whom you enjoy and admire.

You are capable of providing this support for the child in your life who needs it.

So let's get going!

Though it may feel like putting out
a fire, parenting an angry child is much
more like growing a tree.

1

Understanding Anger

Everyone feels angry at times. We feel angry when we're afraid we can't get or might lose something we value, either tangible or intangible. For example, if you have money set aside for a new dress for a special occasion and instead have to spend it on a broken water heater, you may feel frustration or anger. If your boss publicly criticizes you, you may become angry at the loss of dignity and respect in your workplace.

Anger is a valuable aid when we need an adrenaline rush to protect ourselves or others. You may become angry when someone tries to hurt you or someone you care about. If you were grabbed by a stranger, your anger would help you react quickly and aggressively to defend yourself.

Anger can also propel us out of circumstances that are unhealthy, such as an abusive relationship. Like the rising mercury in a thermometer, it can warn us when there may be a problem we need to solve, or a deep emotional issue that needs attention.

Primary feelings come before anger

In spite of its benefits, anger can be an uncomfortable emotion. It is often expressed in unhealthy ways, and can become destructive or dangerous. Dealing with it is complicated by the fact that it is seldom the primary, or first, feeling we have. Anger usually *follows* another feeling, making it the secondary feeling. Before we feel angry, we usually feel vulnerable in some other way, perhaps disappointed or embarrassed. Consider the examples below.

Primary Versus Secondary Feelings

Event	Primary Feeling or Thought	Secondary Feeling or Thought
Karen's boss tells her that her recent marketing proposal was unacceptable.	Hurt, embarrassed, worried: "I'm not skilled enough at my job. What if I get fired?"	Anger: "That guy has always been out to get me. He doesn't even know how hard I work. He's such a jerk."
Jakob, age 11, doesn't get chosen for the baseball team.	Disappointed: "I really wanted to be on that team. I'm no good."	Anger: "The coach's son made it on the team, and I'm way better than him. I hate that kid."
Emily, age 8, doesn't get invited to her classmate's birthday party.	Sad: "I thought those girls liked me. I feel left out."	Anger: "They're stupid. I'm not inviting them to my skating party."
Five-year-old Miguel's brother, wearing a mask, jumps out from behind the couch and yells, "Boo!"	Scared: "There's a monster in here that might hurt me!"	Anger: "My brother is so mean. He wanted to make me cry."
TeLeisha, age 3, is taken to child care for the first time.	Worried: "When is my mommy coming back? What if she forgets me?"	Anger (at child care provider): "Let me go! You're not my mommy!"

As you see, each person felt a different emotion before feeling angry. The transition from the first feeling (primary feeling) to anger (secondary feeling) happens in a split second, usually completely outside of a person's awareness, especially in children. Whether this shift from primary to secondary emotions is instinctual or cultural, most of us are not very comfortable with our vulnerable, primary emotions for many reasons. We may feel less in charge or less safe. We may want to save face or protect ourselves by striking back at those who hurt us.

Many people view anger as a strong, powerful emotion, whereas the primary emotions are often seen as weaknesses. In American culture, boys in particular routinely get the message that anger is the only acceptable emotion to express.

Anger often covers up these primary emotions:

• sadness	• confusion	• impatience
• fear	• disappointment	• rejection
• hurt	• feeling left out	• frustration
• powerlessness	• concern	• worry
• loneliness	• overwhelmed	• embarrassment

WHY IS ANGER DIFFICULT FOR CHILDREN?

Children struggle with anger because they lack life experience, frustration tolerance, impulse control, feelings vocabulary, and problem-solving skills. Each of these factors does its part to help people manage anger in healthy ways.

Life experience

Children may appear to overreact to a situation for sheer lack of understanding that something good may happen. A two-year-old who is asked to share a toy doesn't have enough experience to know that the toy will at some point be returned to him. From our adult perspective, we may think, "Why is he being so dramatic? Why can't he just share?" But, due to lack of experience, he mentally and emotionally believes that if the toy is not in his hands, it is lost forever. No wonder he screams!

Frustration tolerance

Children often cannot recognize the physiological changes in the body that let them know they are in distress. Before they can act on that information, they become flooded with intense emotion. Since they also have few skills to self-soothe, they cannot even begin to respond calmly before they are overwhelmed.

Impulse control

Most parents know that children are not born with the ability to think before acting. Even with the most effective teaching, support, and application of consequences, it takes a long time for children to learn the skills and acquire the maturity needed to manage their impulses. The combination of low frustration tolerance and lack of impulse control causes an angry child to quickly lose control.

Feelings vocabulary

Since children often lack the words to define and label their emotions, they are more likely to resort to physical means to express them. A child may feel extremely disappointed when her mother tells her she cannot have a second cookie. If she is unable to say, "I'm disappointed—I really want another cookie," she will still find a way to communicate that emotion, though it may be in the form of a tantrum or aggression.

Problem-solving skills

All children benefit from learning to solve problems effectively. Imagine a child who has learned to manage his impulses, verbalize his feelings, and self-soothe, but still doesn't know how to solve the problem. If his problem is that his brother took his truck, he may still choose to hit, only because he cannot come up with other solutions. Problem solving requires the ability to identify the problem, think of alternatives, and choose a reasonable one. The following exercise will remind you how complicated anger management is, even for adults.

Exercise: How Skillfully Do You Manage Anger?

Think about a time recently when you felt angry, and answer the following questions.

1. What was the situation?
2. What was your primary feeling or thought?
3. What was your secondary feeling or thought?
4. What did you say and do?
5. Identify as many skills as you can that helped you deal with the situation: life experience, frustration tolerance, impulse control, feeling vocabulary, problem-solving skills.

Follow-up: Did you use all the skills? Did you use them to your satisfaction?

Probably not. These skills are even harder for your child to apply. Remember to be patient as he or she learns how, and patient with yourself as you strengthen your own skills. (See Appendix G for a reproducible worksheet.)

HOW DOES DEVELOPMENT AFFECT ANGER?

The more we understand what normal expression of anger looks like for children at varying stages of development, the better we are able to see that nothing is "wrong" with them when they act their age. As parents, if we always become distressed by our children's expression of anger, rather than seeing it as normal for their age, we are more likely to become angry ourselves, *inadvertently reinforcing the very behavior we are concerned about in them.* For example, it is normal for a four-year-old to get frustrated and shove her two-year-old sister out of her way. Knowing this may help you manage your frustration and concern. Instead of becoming angry yourself, you can teach and model the coping skills you want your child to develop.

"The Face of Anger at Each Developmental Stage," Appendix A, shows what is normal from infancy through middle childhood (twelve years). Look at your child's current stage, and also at the stages before and after. Focus on your child's developmental or emotional age, rather than her chronological age, as children will move through these stages at their own pace regardless of their age. Pay particular attention to how your role as parent changes as your child grows: giving too much or too little support can be frustrating for both you and your child.

WHAT ARE THE SIGNS OF A SERIOUS ANGER PROBLEM?

From time to time every child has an outrageous meltdown. So how do you decide whether your child has an anger problem, or is simply experiencing normal expressions of anger for his age? Taking into account the child's developmental stage, the key factors separating normal and problem anger are *frequency, intensity,* and *severity*, as shown below.

Normal Versus Problem Anger

Frequency	Intensity	Severity
How often does this child have tantrums compared to what is normal for his or her developmental stage?	Does the strength of the emotional expression seem in proportion to the frustrating event? What about the duration of the tantrum? How loud is the child? How much energy is she or he putting into it?	Does this child destroy property or hurt himself or others?
A two-year-old who has daily tantrums would be well within the normal range, but a ten-year-old who shows the same behavior has a problem.	A nine-year-old who rages at the top of her lungs for two hours after being reminded that bedtime is coming up in fifteen minutes (as usual) is an intense child, with intense reactions.	A seven-year-old who routinely hits his mother, throws toys, bangs his head on the floor, or kicks the dog shows severe expression of anger.

If after considering frequency, intensity, and severity, you think your child's behavior is extreme (outside the normal range), you can gather information by asking yourself and others who know him or her the following questions:

- Does my child's angry behavior look different from his peers'?
- Does my child's expression of anger stand out as the only intense part of his personality, or is he intense about everything?
- Has my child's teacher or child care provider expressed concern?
- Is my child's behavior within or outside what's considered normal child development?
- Do my child's peers avoid him?
- Is my child harming property, himself, or others in an extreme way?
- Does my child appear depressed?
- Do I react angrily when my child is angry?

Follow your parental instinct. If you are concerned, seek help from your child's doctor or a mental health professional. (See chapter eight for more information on when to seek professional expertise.)

In this chapter, we have talked about anger, its expression, and what influences it in a child. You have some guidelines to use in deciding whether your child's angry behavior is normal or extreme. In chapter two, we will consider the influence of the child's larger environment.

POINTS TO REMEMBER

- Anger is normal and can be valuable.
- Anger is especially difficult for children to deal with.
- Seek professional help if your situation is extreme.

2

What Makes Kids Angry?

A child's anger is fueled by many things. Here, we will focus on his development, his family, and the broader environment. The distinctions among the three are somewhat artificial, given that these areas are interrelated: what happens in one area impacts each of the others.

You may be tempted to focus solely on your child's angry behavior, especially when it is extreme and contributing to family stress. However, it is essential that you look more broadly because the behavior may be a symptom of problems within the family or the child's environment. Though it can be difficult and uncomfortable, it is important that you recognize, and to the best of your ability, address family and environmental issues that are contributing to your child's behavior before you expect her to change herself.

First, do what you can to reduce the reasons a child may be angry. Then you can use the skills presented in later chapters to help your child deal with any anger that remains.

Influences on a Child's Anger

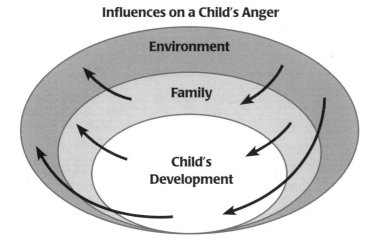

Child-centered sources of anger

Basic needs. Is your child tired? Hungry? Coming down with a cold? Has he been cooped up in the house or the car too long? Often the hallmark of a child whose basic needs require tending is his total lack of reason and control. He obviously needs something, but no strategy you try is right, and, in fact, everything you do throws him further into a rage.

Through the course of a busy day, we often forget to consider the most obvious explanation for challenging behavior. For example, it's ten minutes into a full-blown tantrum before you notice that the time is 1:30 P.M. and your toddler hasn't yet had lunch. Or while traveling to visit Grandma, you are irritated by the fighting in the backseat—until you realize that your four-year-old and seven-year-old have been sitting for three hours straight. Before you dig for deep meaning in your child's behavior, consider the possibility that tending to basic needs may solve the problem.

How Brain Wiring Impacts Anger

Issue	Child's Behavior	Impact on Child's Anger
Active Alert or Spirited Child Temperament	Is more intense, rigid, and persistent	May become angry more easily and have more difficulty calming down. Tantrums may be intense and long lasting
Sensory Problems	Is highly sensitive to sights, sounds, touch, and experiences	May already be highly frustrated most of the time and will be easily upset by issues that seem trivial to adults
Language Delay	Has limited vocabulary; is slower to process information	May not be able to express emotions verbally at time of distress
Attention/ Hyperactivity Disorder	Has difficulties with attention and impulse control	May not be able to slow down enough (mentally or physically) to consider alternatives to aggression
Anxiety and Mood Disorders	May over- or under-respond to experiences; may be inflexible, controlling, or irritable	May already be living with a high level of depression, anxiety, or frustration, so has little tolerance for other day-to-day problems
Fetal Alcohol Effects/Syndrome	Struggles with cause and effect; difficulty reading social cues and getting along in social situations	May have similar difficulties to children with ADHD; may also have difficulty applying skills learned in one area to another
Pervasive Developmental Delays: Asperger's, Autism, etc.	Will most likely experience some or all of the problems listed above	Will likely experience some or all of the problems listed above

Note: For more detailed information on these or other related concerns, see Recommended Reading, page 134, for resources to consult.

Health. Any time a child's behavior is a problem, it is important to consult your child's primary physician to rule out health-related causes for the behavior. There are many medical issues whose symptoms may cause moodiness, irritability, and decreased impulse control or frustration tolerance. For example, a child who is hypoglycemic (has low blood sugar) may appear to be more irrational and irritable. Once a parent is aware of the problem, changes can be made to diet and meal schedules before going to work on behavior.

A child who is sensitive to certain foods or elements in the environment may appear to suffer from attention deficit and anger issues, and again, proper medical treatment may eliminate poor behavior. It would be extremely frustrating to both parent and child, not to mention ineffective, to spend months or years treating a medical concern as if it were solely a behavioral or mental health problem.

Development and temperament. Every child comes into the world genetically predisposed to certain ways of developing and responding to the world around her. Many parents refer to this as how their child is "wired." Areas considered part of your child's wiring are *development, neurological disorders,* and *temperament.* The chart opposite lists some of the more challenging possibilities among the three and a brief description of how each may affect your child's ability to manage and express anger appropriately. Certainly we have not listed every possible concern, but these will give you some ideas of what to look for.

As you know, part of the art of parenting is understanding and responding to the complexities of each individual child's wiring. There are as many different combinations of development, neurological quirks, and temperament as there are children. When a child is diagnosed with a specific developmental or mental health concern, it is important to gather information and seek support and guidance.

This knowledge, combined with your intuition, will enable you to respond to your child in a helpful manner when he is intensely emotional.

Early life experiences. A child is shaped profoundly by what happens early in life. Little is to be gained by looking back on your child's early years with regret. However, there is value in understanding how a child's early life may have shaped his or her way of responding to the world.

None of us had perfect childhoods, nor are any of us capable of protecting our children from every possible bad experience. Each of us brings our own baggage to our parenting. Our parenting styles are based in part on how healthy our relationships with our own parents were, and in part on how our personality developed within those relationships. As we parent, we try to make sense of our experience growing up, and we attempt to improve upon it for our children. Simply put, we do the best we can with what we know.

Of course, every family experiences life circumstances over which we have little or no control. Among these are accidents, illness, and death. The best we can do, then, is to find healthy ways to cope or grieve ourselves, be sensitive to how the event affects our children, and reach out for help and support of others when we need it. Chapter six offers insight and practical ideas for helping children deal with challenging or traumatic situations beyond their control.

Attachment. What a child believes about herself, positively or negatively, results from her early experiences. The health and security of a child's relationship with her parents (or whoever her caregivers may be) directly affect her lifelong ability to give and receive love, express and tolerate emotions (including anger), and develop strong self-esteem. We call this *attachment*.

Attachment is formed by hundreds of thousands of interactions between parent and child beginning from birth.

Eye contact, joyfulness, emotional attunement, playfulness, dependability and structure, and even gentle challenge can foster attachment. The reality of life is that no parent is able to provide all of this, all of the time. However, the more predictable and positive these interactions between parent and child are, the healthier the attachment between them. Look at "Factors that May Affect Attachment," Appendix B, for more information.

Research has shown that children who are insecure or ambivalent toward their parents or caregivers—that is, those with weak attachment—have difficulty managing and expressing emotions later in life. This often results in defiant or angry behavior. On the positive side, children with secure attachments are more likely to develop high self-esteem, get along well with others, and be able to show empathy. If you recognize that your child did not form a secure attachment early on, you have another piece of information to guide you in understanding his or her anger.

Family-centered sources of anger

It is often said that children are resilient. In fact, children are amazing in their ability to survive various stresses and traumas that occur within families. The problem is that children's personalities and characters must form around these unhealthy experiences. For example, a child whose mother is often angry and controlling learns that he cannot get his needs met in straightforward, assertive ways. Instead, he learns to be manipulative. A child who lives with a severely depressed father may learn that in order to get his attention, she must act out. A child who has been abused and neglected as an infant may decide that it is safer to push relationships away.

The situations below illustrate experiences that would have a significant negative impact on a child's development over time. Consider each of the examples and questions to understand the negative ideas each child may be learning about him- or herself, family, and the world.

Situation: Lisa and her son Heath, age 4, at the toy store

Heath: "I want that Power Ranger!"

Lisa: "No, we're here to get a toy for Liam's birthday."

Heath: "But I want that Power Ranger!" [Begins to throw a tantrum. After several minutes of this, Lisa becomes angry and yells.]

Lisa: "Stop being such a brat!" [Slaps Heath across the back of his legs. Heath screams louder. Lisa remembers that her mother used to handle her in this same way, and she had sworn she would do things differently. Lisa kneels down next to Heath.]

Lisa: "Mommy's so sorry, honey. Do you want to pick out a dinosaur?"

- What does Heath learn about dealing with his anger and expressing anger or frustration in front of his mother?
- What does Heath learn about what kind of behavior will get him what he wants in the future?
- Why do you think Lisa becomes verbally abusive when she's angry, and then switches to overindulging her son?

Situation: Dennis and Jill having dinner with their children

The family begins to discuss finances, and Dennis becomes angry at Jill for spending extra money on clothes.

Dennis: "What the hell were you thinking? We can't afford that! You are so stupid sometimes."

Jill: "Dennis, you don't have to be such a jerk about it. Just calm down."

Dennis: [Slamming his fist on the table, and yelling] "I am so sick of being the only responsible one around here." [Jill begins to cry and leaves the table. Dennis turns to the children.]

Dennis: "Seriously, if it wasn't for me, we'd end up living on the street."

- What are the kids likely to be feeling about their parents' relationship?
- What values about communicating feelings and problem solving are the parents transmitting to their children through this type of exchange?
- Loving both parents as children do, how are these children going to figure out how to act toward each parent?

Situation: Leslie and daughters Kylie, age 4, and Hailey, age 7
Leslie, single and committed to providing her girls with the best, works in a high-pressure job and sometimes uses alcohol to "take the edge off." After a particularly stressful day, she drinks a bottle of wine with dinner. The bedtime routine with Kylie doesn't go smoothly or quickly, and Kylie keeps getting up after being put to bed. Exhausted and out of patience, Leslie becomes angry.
Leslie: "You get back in that bed! I'm sick and tired of you getting up all the time when you know you're supposed to stay in bed!" [Hits Kylie, who starts crying. Hailey runs into the living room and shuffles Kylie off to her own bedroom.]
Hailey: "Don't worry, Mommy. I'll help Kylie go to sleep." [The next day Leslie recognizes that scenes like last night's are happening more and more often.]

- What are Kylie and Hailey learning about how to handle stress?
- How might repeated experiences of this nature affect their feelings and behavior in the future?
- What might happen if Leslie continues to explode unpredictably?

The situations above illustrate that parenting is about much more than possessing a set of skills to manage children's behavior. How adults model expression of feelings, how healthy their marital and parenting relationships are, and how they solve conflicts are equally powerful as teachers as whatever technique they use to discipline their children. Each significantly impacts how a child experiences and expresses anger.

Environment-based factors

Media. Today more than ever, parents have to deal with the media's influence on their children. Of the hundreds of television channels that families have available for viewing in their homes, many have mature and violent scenes depicted during children's waking hours. Young children are most vulnerable to the effects of media violence. They are more impressionable, have a harder time distinguishing between fantasy and reality, learn by observing and imitating, and cannot easily discern motives for violence. The American Academy of Pediatrics and five other prominent medical groups warn of the following effects of media violence on children:

- increased antisocial and aggressive behavior
- desensitization to violence and those who suffer from violence
- increased desire to see more violence in entertainment and real life
- view that violence is an acceptable way to settle conflicts

(Source: Congressional Public Health Summit, 2000)

With the many stresses of parenting, it is easy to become complacent about policing children's television viewing. Between the bombardment of inappropriate media accessible to children and the social pressures upon parents to allow children to view whatever is popular at the moment, you may find yourself giving in and saying, "Oh, it probably won't cause any permanent damage." However, the research regarding media violence and its impact on children certainly makes a strong argument to the contrary.

Just as you would want to be sure that your children get healthy food and good educational experiences, it is important that you make purposeful decisions about your family values regarding media. While limiting your children's exposure to harmful media may feel inconvenient, the guidelines and values that you teach them regarding media will have a lasting impact on their development, *especially on their ability to manage anger in healthy and safe ways.*

Schools, child care, and peers. While you as the parent have the most power to shape your child's values and behaviors, another important influence throughout her life will be her peers. Being aware of your child's social environment at school, child care, and in your neighborhood is an important part of parenting. While most parents hope to raise children who are kind, accepting, and able to get along with a wide range of people, we also recognize that children often emulate the unacceptable behavior and attitudes of some of their peers.

When you are aware of your child's social environment, you will be better equipped to guide and set limits for your child. In some situations you will use a peer's unhealthy decisions as an opportunity to discuss your family's values and how those might help your child make healthy decisions. At other times you will decide your child cannot continue to associate with another child, or perhaps you will allow the association only under your watchful eye. While your child may resent you for not allowing association with certain peers, at some level she can also recognize that you are being loving and protective by providing boundaries.

In chapter two, we have talked about the different sources of children's anger, from temperament and development to the environment. In chapter three, we will focus on helping children understand, express, and deal with their feelings.

POINTS TO REMEMBER

- Unsatisfied basic needs can lead to anger and can usually be taken care of easily.
- A child's anger is affected by health and development, family and environment.
- Temperament influences how a child expresses anger.

3

Dealing with Feelings

While it is important to know what to do to help your child when she becomes emotionally or physically out of control, taking the initiative to teach your child about her emotions "behind the scenes"—in between her angry bouts—is far more effective than anything you can do in the moment of an angry outburst. In this chapter we will focus on the skills that help children to recognize, identify, and express their feelings.

The first step to help your child manage intense feelings is to consistently show behavior you want to see by:

- Modeling: Set a good example.
- Teaching: Teach what you want to see at a neutral time when the child is not angry or in conflict.
- Coaching: Help your child apply what you've taught when he or she is angry or having trouble.

EXPRESSING PRIMARY FEELINGS

Learning to *express primary feelings* yourself is one of the ways of modeling for your children the healthy expression of emotions. Many parents find using primary feeling language somewhat awkward, even a bit silly at first. However, with practice, we assure you it will become second nature. And, fortunately, your children will learn this new language simply by hearing you use it. If your family doesn't speak the language of primary feelings, it's time to learn. Consider the two contrasting examples below, one skipping over the primary emotion and the other using primary feeling language.

Situation: Joshua, age 8, and his mother at the grocery store

Example 1

Joshua: "Mom, I want a candy bar."

Mom: "No, you've already had too much sugar."

Joshua: [whining] "But, Mooommmm . . . "

Mom: [irritated] "Stop it! I don't want to hear it."

Joshua: [yelling] "You never let me have anything. You're so mean!"

Mom: [threatening] "Watch it, you are walking a thin line. . . . "

Joshua: [screaming and kicking at the grocery cart] "Aaarrrghh!"

Example 2

Joshua: "Mom, I want a candy bar."

Mom: "Not today, honey."

Joshua: [whining] "But, Mooommmm . . . "

Mom: "You sound disappointed. I know that's your favorite candy."

Joshua: "Why can't I have it just this once?"

Mom: "I'm worried that you've already had too much sugar today."

Joshua: [disappointed, but resigned—voice calm] "Ugh—Mom, you're so strict!"

Mom: "I know it's hard not getting what you want."
[Mom then turns and pays the cashier for the groceries.]

In the first example, Joshua responds to his mother's "no" by whining, rather than expressing his primary feeling of disappointment. Then, instead of helping Joshua label his disappointed feeling, his mother expresses irritation at his whining, and tells him to stop expressing any thoughts or feelings at all. Joshua becomes angry, and his mother responds further by threatening him. Beyond the negativity of the interaction, the intensity of his mother's reaction to Joshua's anger actually reinforces it, making it more likely that he will become angry next time.

In the second example, Joshua's mother responds to his whining by labeling what is most likely his primary emotion in that moment—disappointment—and providing some level of understanding about why he might be feeling that way. She expresses her own primary feeling of being worried that he has had too much sugar already. This helps him understand how she's thinking and feeling, and models the primary feeling of "worried" that he may be able to use himself in a situation some time in the future. By giving him the word "disappointed" at the moment he is feeling it, Joshua's mother helps him make the connection between what he is experiencing and how he might verbalize that feeling in the future.

Empathizing

Many parents are concerned that if they take the time to label and empathize with primary emotions, it will cause their kids to become *more* whiny. They equate empathizing with giving in and becoming lenient. However, the opposite is true: labeling and empathizing with kids' feelings lets them know that their feelings are important, gives them an opportunity to build a vocabulary for expressing their feelings, and lays the foundation for emotional maturity. Empathizing is about supporting a child through his or her emotional response to your limit, not changing that limit in order rescue the child (and you!) from the emotion. At no time does empathizing with your child mean adjusting, or backing down on, a limit that you have decided is best for your child.

The other benefit of empathizing with a child's emotions rather than responding with your own anger is that it keeps the focus where it belongs: on the issue. When a parent remains calm, the child is allowed to experience his own emotions (and any consequences that may be associated). If a parent responds in anger, the child is more likely to focus his energy toward being angry at his parent. Suddenly the original issue is lost, and in its place stress is created in the relationship between parent and child.

HOW TO BUILD A FEELINGS VOCABULARY

Parents spend a great deal of time building their children's vocabulary. We teach them to label their body parts, animals, letters, numbers, and colors. These are certainly important for them to know so they can communicate with others. However, more important than being taught the word *cow* is for a child to be taught words like *sad, frustrated, disappointed, worried,* or *scared* so he can begin to communicate his inner life. When it comes to getting along in the world, the ramifications of getting frustrated and not being able to communicate it without violence are serious.

Opportunities to begin teaching feelings language start from day one. Obviously a crying infant does not understand the words, but a parent who verbalizes and uses a congruent facial expression while saying, "Oh, my, you look frustrated!" begins not only to prepare the child to learn this language, but also gets herself in the habit of offering it. Throughout your child's day, there are countless opportunities in which you can model feelings words, label your child's and others' feelings, and offer empathy to encourage the expression of feelings.

The good news about labeling primary feelings is twofold: it is one of the most powerful things you can do to improve your child's ability to manage difficult emotions, and it is also the simplest. You don't need a curriculum or flash cards, you need only to seize the daily teachable moments.

Teach word and expression

When Rachel plays with Eli, her one-year-old, she makes a game out of showing exaggerated facial expressions and naming the corresponding feelings (happy, sad, surprised, scared, mad, etc.). Eli loves this game, and now will animatedly show the expression on his face when Rachel says the feeling word.

"I feel ... "

Ask child to think about feelings

Three-year-old Frank and his father, Ted, read story books every night before bed. While they are reading, Ted often takes the time to point out or question how characters might be feeling at critical story points. For example, "Oh, Frank, how do you think Max felt when Chris took his blocks?"

Show child how to recognize another's feelings

Janie, age 6, was playing with her friend Tess, and grabbed Tess's doll out of her hand without asking. Janie's mother stepped in and encouraged Janie to look at Tess's face and see if she could tell how she was feeling. Janie looked, and then said, "She's sad and mad because I took her doll."

Model how to label one's feelings

Tami is driving in rush-hour traffic with her 12-year-old son Gregory in the backseat. Several things have gone wrong in the day, and she is becoming irritable. When another driver cuts her off, she wants to yell. Instead, she begins to verbalize her primary emotions, saying, "You know, Gregory, I am really feeling frustrated. This day just has not gone how I wanted it to. I was really hoping for you and me to spend the day doing something fun, and I am so disappointed that my errands and the traffic are getting in the way of that. I feel like I just want to scream, but I think I'm going to put on some music and take some deep breaths. Sound like a plan?"

In each of the examples above, the parent took the opportunity to label, express, or discuss primary emotions related to the situation. Each discussion was simple and took less than two minutes, but served the important purpose of building the child's awareness of and ability to express a wide range of feelings.

Basic Feelings Vocabulary

Start with the basic four emotions of happy, sad, scared, and mad, and then add these words as your child's vocabulary grows.

• content	• pleased	• excited	• terrified
• annoyed	• frustrated	• furious	• hurt
• embarrassed	• disappointed	• unhappy	• loving
• curious	• proud	• silly	• left out
• surprised	• worried	• afraid	• confused

By using primary feelings language in your family and building your child's feelings vocabulary, you are laying the foundation for your child to be successful in dealing with intense emotions *as they happen.*

Typically developing children progress from crying or raging as toddlers, to physical outburst, to verbal expression of how they are feeling. Based on their maturity level or what had been modeled for them in their environment, children may begin verbalizing their feelings in ways that are unacceptable. Phrases like "I hate you," "You're stupid," "Shut up," "I'm going to kill you," or worse are probably not how you would choose to have your child express intense emotion. At the same time, the fact that your child is choosing words rather than physical aggression is progress in the right direction.

Talk with your kids about your values concerning verbal aggression during periods of calm, and make it clear what is acceptable in your family. Be sure you coach your child in using appropriate ways to express feelings with primary emotions language at the time he or she is upset.

If your child is verbally aggressive, you can use a time-out to allow her to calm down, just as you might if she were physically aggressive. (See chapter four for more information on using time-outs effectively.) Other times you may recognize the child's verbal aggression as an attempt to distract you from the issue at hand and choose to ignore it. For example, a young child who tries out a curse word or an older child who shouts, "I hate you" when you've set a limit might be better ignored at that moment, so as not to reinforce the behavior.

USING AND TEACHING YOUR CHILD TO USE I-MESSAGES

I-messages are a basic and very effective communication tool that can be used by anyone to communicate in a clear, honest, and assertive way. The format of an I-message is particularly effective because it:

- allows the speaker to take ownership of his feelings without blame
- connects the feelings to what is happening at the time
- ends with a clear statement as to the speaker's wants or needs

I-Message

"I feel . . .
when . . .
because . . .
I would like . . . "

Be sure to use a primary feeling word in the "I feel . . . " part, rather than variations of "angry," the secondary or cover-up emotion.

In the "I would like" section, state your wish positively, rather than negatively. For example, instead of "I would like you to quit hitting your sister," say, "I would like you to use nice hands with your sister" or "I would like you to use words with your sister."

Using I-messages is one of the most effective ways you can help your child begin to communicate primary emotions. As with many of the other new skills presented in this book, you may feel awkward when you first begin using them, but as you become more practiced and comfortable with them, they will come naturally to you. There are many opportunities for you to both model and teach I-messages during the course of an average day. The following examples illustrate a few.

Situation: Oliver, age 3, climbing the bookshelf

Mom: "Oliver, *I feel* worried *when* you climb the bookshelf *because* I'm scared you might fall and get hurt. *Please keep your feet on the floor.*"

Note that for a preschooler, you may be walking toward him and assisting him to get down at the same time as you are saying this, and that you may shorten the length of the statement, if needed. For example, you may instead say, "I'm scared you might fall down. Please put your feet on the floor."

Situation: Meg, age 9, listening to parents, John and Nancy

John: [looking into the refrigerator] "Why don't we ever have any milk in this house?"

Nancy: [looking irritated and defensive] "I haven't had a chance to get to the store yet."
John: "Is something wrong?"
Nancy: "Well, *I feel* hurt *when* you ask the question that way *because* it feels like you're suggesting I never do my job. *It would feel better to me if* you would either supportively let me know we're out of milk so I can get it next time I'm at the store, or offer to go to the store for some milk yourself."

Situation: Jason, age 7, playing with his friend Trevor

Jason: [angrily] "Hey! Why did you take the Legos I was using?"
Trevor: "I need them for my spaceship!"
Jason: "I was using them!" [yanks back the Legos, breaking Trevor's spaceship]
Mom: [comes near, crouching between the two boys] "It looks like you two have a problem. Jason, can you use your words to let Trevor know how you felt when he took your Legos?"
Jason: "Trevor, *I felt* disappointed when you took my Legos *because* I needed them for my tower. *I would like you* to ask first next time."
Trevor: "Okay, I will."
Mom: "Thank you, Jason, for using your words with Trevor. Trevor, can you let Jason know how you felt when Jason broke your spaceship when he was taking back the pieces?"
Trevor: "Jason, *I felt* sad when you broke my spaceship *because* I worked really hard on it. *Next time,* can you ask for them back instead of grabbing them?"
Jason: "Sorry, I didn't mean to break it."

The preceding examples may seem unrealistic as they are simplified here for the purpose of explanation. While they learn, children will need coaching to say each individual part of the I-message. In fact, you may be separating two angry children who are about to become physical with each other, while assisting them to verbalize primary feelings. The less mature or more angry the child, the messier this process can look in the early stages. Sometimes you will feel as if you were only marginally successful. However, if parents model using I-messages themselves and coach children to use them, children will eventually trust the process, and, yes, even learn to do it independently.

USING ACTIVE LISTENING

Active listening is a technique for helping another person clarify his feelings. It reflects both the feeling and the content of the other person's message (both verbal and nonverbal). This accomplishes three things: it continues to build your child's vocabulary of primary feelings words, it gives her the opportunity to apply the vocabulary to an actual situation, and most importantly, it communicates to your child that her feelings matter to you.

Active listening can be used both when a child is first becoming upset in order to help prevent further loss of control, as well as to calm down a child who has already begun to lose control. It is helpful because it gives a child who is either too young or too flooded with emotion assistance in recognizing, identifying, and expressing his feelings.

Consider the following example illustrating a parent responding to a child who is just beginning to become upset.

Situation: Sam, age 9, and his mother at the video store
Example 1
Sam: "Let's get this movie!"
Mom: "Remember, the family rule is that until you are 13 you can choose G- or PG-rated movies."
Sam: "C'mon mom, all the other kids get to watch PG-13 movies!"
Mom: "That may be, but this is our rule."
Sam: [slams down the movie, yelling] "This is so stupid. Everyone else gets to. I hate our family!"
Mom: "Quit making such a big deal about this. I'm sure

you can find something else you'd like."

Sam: [folds arms angrily against chest and kicks at the floor] "Then I don't want any movie!"

Mom: "Fine, if you want to throw a fit instead of get a movie, then we won't get one!"

Sam: [storming out of the video store] "I hate you!"

Example 2

Sam: "Let's get this movie!"

Mom: "Remember, the family rule is that until you are 13 you can choose G- or PG-rated movies."

Sam: "C'mon mom, all the other kids get to watch PG-13 movies!"

Mom: "I'm sure it's frustrating if you feel our family rule is different from some of your friends'."

Sam: [slams down the movie, yelling] "This is so stupid. Everyone else gets to. I hate our family!"

Mom: "It sounds like you were really hoping I'd change the rule this time. I can understand why you're disappointed."

Sam: [sulks for a few moments. Mom gives him some time to sit with his feelings.]

Mom: [supportively] "Are you feeling like you're ready to choose a movie, or are you not sure you want to get a movie, after all?"

Sam: [sighs] "No, I want to pick a movie—but I still really hate this rule."

Mom: "I'm impressed with how you managed the big feelings you had, and still were able to make a decision that works for you."

In the first example, Mom restates the rule, but then misses an opportunity to help Sam label and process his feelings, insisting that he instead "quit making a big deal." Sam responds to this with increased anger. Understandably frustrated, Mom matches his anger, and they both leave the movie store angry.

In the second example, Mom also restates the family

rule. However, when Sam continues to argue and get angry, Mom reflects both his feelings and the situation through active listening by noting Sam's frustration with the rule, but doesn't get caught up arguing with his assertion that "everyone else gets to," or in her internal reaction to his button-pushing statement of "I hate this family." Mom recognizes that it is normal for his anger to continue to a degree, even though she is reflecting his feelings, and continues to draw his attention to his disappointment about the rule, rather than joining him in his anger. She allows him time to "sit with" his feelings, neither attempting to rescue him from them or demand that he stop feeling them. She then gives him a chance to come to his own decision, and acknowledges his ability to return to being calm and make a decision that works for him.

The key difference between the first and second examples is that in the first, Sam not only does not learn how to manage and express his feelings of disappointment, he and his mother remain angry and emotionally estranged from each other over the situation. In the second example, Sam learns more about having and labeling his primary feelings, and experiences his mother as loving and supportive even as she assertively guards family rules.

Active listening with an out-of-control child

Active listening is a powerful tool to use with a child who has already launched into a full-blown angry outburst. In these situations, active listening extends beyond building your child's vocabulary of primary feelings words. You give him the chance to apply his vocabulary to the situation. At the same time you communicate that you care about his strong emotions. In this way you guide the child through what can be a frightening situation—the feeling of being out of control.

As adults, we sometimes discount the intensity behind the feelings a child encounters throughout the course of a typical day. To a two-year-old, losing a toy momentarily to a sibling can feel as intense as if you were to lose your car to a car thief. Asking a six-year-old to end a play date early might be comparable to your having to say good-bye to a family member, not knowing whether you'll see her again for many years. For a twelve-year-old, not being chosen for the baseball team for the second year in a row would feel similar to your being passed over for a promotion in your job every year for the past ten years.

We often view a child's emotional reaction to day-to-day situations through an adult lens, not taking into account his limited experience and maturity. We see his reaction as unreasonable and may belittle his emotional experience, rather than offer him the support and guidance he needs to find his way through the situation emotionally intact and with more skills to handle the next experience he faces. Consider the following examples of a child who becomes emotionally out of control, and the impacts of two contrasting responses from parents.

Situation: Kimberly, age 4, asking to go on an outing

Kimberly, an intense and stubborn child who often loses control emotionally, asks her mother if they can go on a trip to the local water slide. Her mother tells her they have other plans and can't go today.

Example 1
Kimberly: [stomps her feet and yells] "But I want to, I want to!"
Mom: "I said not today."
Kimberly: [throws herself down, crying and screaming]
Mom: "Kimberly, that's enough! I said we're not going today, and I mean it!"
Kimberly: [shrieks and cries even louder]
Mom: "Stop it. If you're going to act like that, go to your room."
Kimberly: [yells even louder and kicks at Mom]
Mom: "That's it!" [Mom angrily picks up a kicking and

screaming Kimberly and takes her to her room] "You can stay here until you stop crying."

Kimberly: [screams and cries in her room for 45 minutes before she finally falls asleep]

Example 2

Kimberly: [stomps her feet and yells] "But I want to, I want to!"

Mom: "I know you're disappointed, honey, but we have other plans."

Kimberly: [throws herself down, crying and screaming]

Mom: [increasing the level of her empathy expressed in her voice tone and facial expression] "I know you really want to go—it's so disappointing. You look really sad and mad."

Kimberly: [still crying and screaming, but not escalating]

Mom: "It's hard when you're hoping for something and it doesn't work out. It's so hot today, it would have been fun to go, wouldn't it?"

Kimberly: [still screaming and crying, but beginning to tune in to what her mother is saying]

Mom: "Wouldn't it be fun if we could go to the water slides EVERY day? We would just spend all of our time there, and go down the really big blue slide with the loops a hundred times. I wish we could do that, too."

Kimberly: [whimpering a bit from having cried so hard] "Yeah, Mommy, that would be fun, I would love to go there everyday. I really want to go. When we do go, could I go on the red slide with the big splashy part? I like that one the best."

Mom: "I know it's sad to not go today. I'm glad you could let me know how you were feeling. And, yes, we should definitely go on the red splashy slide when we go!"

In the first example, Mom is attempting to regain control of the situation by continuing to clarify the limit about going to the water slides and insisting that Kimberly calm down. When this doesn't work, she resorts to threats, which lead to her physically intervening, and then she must wait out a 45-minute screaming tantrum afterwards. Kimberly finally falls asleep, with no resolution to a very angry exchange between her and Mom, and with no additional skills modeled or learned.

In the second example, Kimberly becomes emotional so quickly that Mom is not able to prevent the tantrum. This example demonstrates two ways of using active listening. First, Mom stays disengaged from Kimberly's anger, and describes her guesses about Kimberly's feelings. She continues to calmly verbalize and talk about the situation, despite Kimberly's continued crying. Mom is not agitated by Kimberly's crying, but offers words to help Kimberly begin to label her feelings and to let her know that Mom understands and cares about her feelings.

Second, Mom gives Kimberly in fantasy what she can't have in reality. She does this by talking about the enjoyable things they would be doing at the water slide if they could go. Rather than making Kimberly more upset, this actually calms Kimberly because she feels her mom understands the intensity of her desire to go. In the spirit of building trust, Mom should be sure to take Kimberly to the water slides sometime in the near future.

In this chapter, we have talked about the importance of parents modeling the use of feelings language, as well as teaching children an extensive vocabulary of feelings words they can use to express primary emotions. In chapter four, we will consider a number of self-calming skills kids can use when their feelings run high.

POINTS TO REMEMBER

- Start building a feelings vocabulary at birth.
- Model and teach vocabulary for primary emotions using I-messages.
- Use active listening, a powerful tool to teach and to calm your child.

4

Tools Kids Need to Manage Intense Feelings

The goal of the skills presented in this and following chapters is to help you build an emotionally mature child *over time.* These skills consist of things you can do when the child is angry, as well as skills you can teach in calm times.

It has been our experience in our practice that many times parents will try a new skill for a few weeks, and return discouraged that it "doesn't work." This happens for several reasons. First, if the skill is new to you, it will take time for you to become proficient in teaching the skill to your child. Second, your child will take some time to learn the skill as well. And third, most children respond to change with resistance and limit testing.

It is also important to note that nothing works every time. Frankly, even if you had built all of these skills into your child's life from birth, they still would not work every time. However, if you consistently use these skills and model appropriate behavior in your family, your child will very likely learn over time to express his thoughts and feelings in healthy ways. He is more likely to show empathy in his relationships, be capable of positive problem solving, and feel good about himself and others.

Regardless of how proactive you are at helping your child understand and express his intense feelings, every child will from time to time lose control. Your role at these times is that of coach, reminding him of the skills you have taught and practiced at other calm, neutral times through role plays and modeling.

The following skills for calming oneself are some of our favorite techniques that you can use to coach your child through her anger. Knowing your child's personality and strengths can guide you in choosing those that will be the most effective for her. Just like everything else, know that nothing works immediately or every time. Expect to teach and practice these skills many times before you see your child using them successfully.

TAKE DEEP BREATHS

Teaching children to take deep breaths when they begin to get upset may seem too simple to be effective, but it is a life-long skill for managing stress that has emotional, behavioral, and biological benefits.

- *How to teach it before you need it:* There are many opportunities to teach deep breathing during the course of the day. You can model it: "Oh, dear, I'm so frustrated! I think I'll take a deep breath." You can role play about it: "This dinosaur is disappointed he didn't get to go first—he's going to take three deep breaths to help him calm down."

- *How to coach it in the moment:* Guess what your child is feeling and offer the skill. "Wow, you look like you're getting frustrated with that tower. Now might be a great time for three deep breaths. Let's take them together."

COUNT TO TEN

Counting to ten (or whatever number is developmentally appropriate for your child) has many of the same benefits of deep breaths. The most valuable part of teaching children to count to ten is that it creates a few moments for them to calm down before they react to a situation.

- *How to teach it before you need it:* The same techniques for teaching deep breathing can work for counting to ten. "I'm getting so frustrated! I'm going to count to ten."

  While reading a book, discuss a character's feelings, and comment, "I bet that boy could take a deep breath and count to five to calm down."

  It is always powerful for your children to see you try out a skill: "You know, Justin, Mommy is getting frustrated. I'm going to go count to ten to calm down and then I'll come back and we'll solve this problem."

- *How to coach it in the moment:* "Kaylee, you look pretty angry—do you want to count to five or ten to calm down?"

POSITIVE SELF-TALK

Positive self-talk is a way for kids to *coach themselves*. We know that what we tell ourselves about our situation or our ability to handle it creates our beliefs and has a major impact on what happens next. Coming up with developmentally appropriate positive statements that a child can say or think right after taking deep breaths and counting helps him calm down and eventually be able to problem solve during in the situation.

- *How to teach it before you need it:* You can point out times in real life, the media, sports, or stories when people can give themselves positive messages. "Julian, you know what? I'm getting frustrated trying to make this cake turn out right. I am going to take three deep breaths and count to five. Now I'm going to tell myself, 'I know I can do this. It's okay if it's not perfect.'"

With older children, you can talk about how baseball batters coach themselves after they swing through a strike: "I know I can hit this next ball."

- *How to coach it in the moment:* "James, I know you're disappointed about striking out. I'm so glad you were able to take a deep breath and count to five. Now how about saying to yourself, "I know I'm a good player. Even professional players strike out. I know I can do it next time."

RELAXATION VISUALIZATION

Visualization is the skill of being able to take oneself quickly to a calm place, such as being able to visualize being on a beach, or under a protective tree in some forest, in order to gain a few moments of emotional escape.

- *How to teach it before you need it:* You can take advantage of bedtime, when children often need help to relax to fall asleep. Ask your child to tell you about a place or places where she feels safe and calm. Ask her to paint a picture of that place in her head and imagine herself there. Remind her that this is her special place, and that she can go there any time she is feeling afraid, lonely, angry, etc.

- *How to coach it in the moment:* "Rachel, I can tell you are feeling really overwhelmed. Now might be a great time for you to take a moment to picture that place that makes you feel calm. Do you want to take some time to do that by yourself, or would you like us to draw a picture of your place together?"

POSITIVE OUTCOME VISUALIZATION

This is visualizing a positive outcome to the current difficult situation, such as a child visualizing assertively asking for a turn on the swings rather than shoving his brother off them.

- *How to teach it before you need it:* For a young child who is having trouble waiting his turn at school, you might teach him to create a "mind picture" of himself standing in line for the drinking fountain, singing the ABC song in his head to help him successfully wait his turn. For older children, using an example of sports offers a great opportunity to teach kids about the idea of visualization, because it is a common method used by many of the great coaches. While watching a basketball game, you can talk with your child about the ways that coaches not only teach their players to physically practice skills, but to also visualize themselves making progress and having positive outcomes.

- *How to coach it in the moment:* This skill is best used when a child is relatively calm. Once a child has taken deep breaths and counted to ten, then you can remind him of his visualizing a positive outcome in the past. This may be enough to help him revisit that vision, and attempt to make the vision come true.

VERBALIZE FEELINGS

The skills discussed in chapters three and four—feelings vocabulary, I-messages, and active listening—are skills that help kids calm down.

- *How to teach it before you need it:* Take advantage of opportunities throughout the day to help your child access, identify, and express the emotions he has. Give him the message that all of his feelings are acceptable, even while you limit negative behavior. This encourages verbal expression of feelings, replacing tantrums or aggression.

- *How to coach it in the moment:* "Sally, you look upset. Can you use your words to let Joan know how you're feeling?"

ASK FOR HELP

It's important to remind children, regardless of their age, that it is okay to ask for help. While we all want children to work toward self-mastery, we also need to teach them how and when to reach out.

- *How to teach it before you need it:* One of the most effective ways to teach children that it's okay to ask for help is to model it for them. Be sure that they see you asking others for help when you are frustrated. For example, when you feel you are reaching your limit with an angry child, you might say to your parenting partner, "I'm feeling frustrated right now. Can you please come help Jacob pick up his toys for me?" Then be sure to model an appropriate self-calming method, such as breathing deeply or taking a time-out in your room.

- *How to coach it in the moment:* "Cole, you are looking pretty frustrated with tying that shoe. I noticed you've done a great job taking deep breaths and counting to five. Remember that it's okay to ask for help if you need it."

SAFE WAYS TO EXPEND ANGRY ENERGY

Often children get the message that it's not okay to be angry, rather than the message that there are safe and unsafe ways to express anger. The list below gives an "anger menu" that includes some of the ideas above, as well as other suggestions for children to choose from when they are angry. It can be very helpful to create your own menu with your child, adding pictures, and to post it in your home, so that you can remind your child to use it as a resource when she becomes upset.

Some safe ways to be angry are:
• Take several deep breaths
• Count to 5 or 10
• Draw an "angry" picture and tear it up
• Squish play dough
• Scream into a pillow
• Squeeze, throw, or kick a ball
• Run around outside
• Go for a walk (with an adult)
• Say, "I'm mad because. . . ."
• Take a time-out for yourself

MAKING GOOD DECISIONS WHILE ANGRY

Another important concept for children to learn is that being angry and making a good decision need not be mutually exclusive processes. Learning how to maintain good judgment even when emotion runs high is a sign of maturity. Children can learn over time that they can separate their feelings from their behavior.

Making a good decision may mean taking steps to calm down; other times it may mean making a decision to successfully solve the problem. It is particularly important for children to see you model this skill. And it is one you will want to coach them through often until they get the hang of it. The reinforcement system described in Appendix E will encourage this skill.

USE TIME-OUT POSITIVELY

Time-out first emerged as a tool for parents to use in place of spanking. It was intended to be time spent in a positive place where children could calm down and regain control of their feelings before being redirected to more appropriate behavior. Today, however, it is often used as punishment. When parents say things such as, "If you don't stop that, you're going to get a time-out," children begin to view time-out as being "in trouble," and can no longer see it as a positive tool for regaining self-control. Children are then less likely to be able to take themselves to time-out when they need it.

There are three ways to effectively teach children about positive time-out: through parents modeling using time-out themselves, by teaching children to take themselves to time-out, and by positively assisting them to time-out when appropriate. The goal in each of these, as the following examples will illustrate, is to teach children that time-out is a positive tool for self-calming rather than a punishment.

Time-Out Basics

What is the purpose of a time-out?
- To teach, not to punish
- To provide space for big feelings
- To take a break from a frustrating situation
- To calm down enough to communicate feelings and solve problems

Where should a time-out take place?
- Any place that is safe and relatively quiet or nonstimulating
- As some children will feel abandoned out of sight of their parent, time-out can occur within view of the parent. If a child is unable to stay where you put him or her, refer to "Physically Assisting a Child to Time-Out" on page 52.

How long should a time-out last?
- A reasonable guideline is one minute per year of age, however, many children can calm themselves in less time. Remember that the goal of time-out is to become calm; it is not a punishment and should not go on for long periods.

Parent's modeling time-out

If we expect our children to feel comfortable removing themselves from a distressing situation in order to regain control before problem solving, then we must model that as adults. Sometimes when we are frustrated with them about something they are doing, it is a good time to say, "I am feeling very irritated by what you're doing. I need to take myself to time-out for a few minutes to take deep breaths, count to ten, and think positive thoughts. Then I'll come out and be ready to be the kind of mom I want to be." Then you can go to your room, shut the door, and take the time you need before responding. Children are astute observers, and the fact that you use these skills is the best way for them to be willing to use them, too. The example below shows a father modeling time-out.

Situation: Matthew working on the car with Toby, age 7
Matthew becomes increasingly frustrated as he tries to replace the carburetor. He is very aware of his son's presence and has so far managed not to swear at the car, the carburetor, or the world in general. Matthew realizes that this is a good time to model using time-out—and he sure could use one!
Matthew: "Toby, this darn carburetor is so frustrating. I feel like I want to throw it! I don't think that will solve my problem, though. Instead, I think I'll step away from it for a few minutes and take care of my feelings."
[Matthew steps away, counts slowly out loud to ten, then takes ten deep breaths. He tells Toby that he is going to think of his favorite calm place for a few minutes, and then he says aloud to himself, "I know I can do this. I'm going to try again."]
Matthew: [as he walks back to the car] "Whew! Toby, I feel a lot better now. I think I'm ready to try again. If I'm still having trouble, I'll call Uncle John and see if he can help."

Teaching children to use time-out

As with any new skill, the best time to teach your child about time-out is in a calm, neutral time. In our preschool day treatment program where we served children who desperately needed safe ways to express anger, we regularly presented time-out in circle times as a "gift you can give yourself when you have big feelings" or "a place to take care of big feelings." This can be done through simple, developmentally appropriate explanation and role-play.

The example below describes the way staff role-played and modeled time-out for the children. Once children can take themselves to time-out to calm down, they will be able to use the communication and problem-solving skills that will bring them success in other environments.

Situation: Teachers Karin and Chris model time-out

Teacher Karin: [sitting at the art table with three children] "Aarrrgghh! I can't get this glue bottle open! I feel like throwing it across the room."

Teacher Chris: "Teacher Karin, it looks like you're getting frustrated. Why don't you try taking three deep breaths?" [turning to the kids] "What else can she try, kids?"

Kids: [responding excitedly] "She can count to five!"

Teacher Karin: [feigning hesitancy] "Well, okay, I guess I can try that." [takes three deep breaths and slowly counts to five] "Well, that helped a little, but I still feel kind of frustrated—I still can't get the top off the glue."

Teacher Chris: "Why don't you try telling yourself, 'Calm down. I know I can do this.'"

Teacher Karin: "All right. Calm down—I can do this." [then tries to get the glue bottle open again, but is unsuccessful. Her next response is more intense than the first] "I'm getting so mad! I want to throw this glue bottle against the wall!"

Teacher Chris: "Teacher Karin, it seems like you might need to take a break to calm down."

Teacher Karin: [dramatically yelling as she stomps to the time-out area] "I'm so mad at that stinkin glue!" [while Karin is in the time-out area she quietly but dramatically models deep breathing, counting, and positive self-talk]

Teacher Chris: [to the students] "What do you guys think Teacher Karin is doing right now?"
Kids: [responding excitedly] "She's taking deep breaths." "She's counting to five." "Telling herself to calm down."
Teacher Karin: [walking out of time-out, looking calm, talking to herself] "Well, I counted to 15 because I was pretty frustrated, and then I took five whole deep breaths. I feel better now. I think I'm going to ask for help with that glue bottle."

Physically assisting a child to time-out

When a child has become so overwhelmed with emotion that she cannot take herself to time-out, a parent can physically assist her to time-out. In the spirit of keeping time-out as a positive tool, it can be helpful as you take her to time-out to verbalize to the child phrases such as, "You're not in trouble; you just need to take care of your (sad, mad, disappointed, frustrated) feelings for a few minutes," or "It's okay to be mad, and it's not okay to hit your brother. Let's take a few minutes until you find your control again."

When physically assisting a child to time-out, the following elements are important to keep in mind:

1. Once you have made the decision that a child needs to be assisted to time-out, and have communicated that to the child, do not negotiate further. At the last minute, many children will attempt to talk you out of taking them to time-out. It is important to follow through, so that you don't establish a pattern of negotiating once you've set a limit about offering parental assistance.

2. When assisting a child to time-out, it is important to verbalize what you are doing and why by saying phrases such as, "It looks like you need some help regaining your control." However, it is essential that you refrain from any other comments or discussion, either positive or negative, as this may actually reinforce negative behavior. Remember that your goal in assisting your child

to time-out is to send a message that time-out is a safe, useful, and nonpunitive experience, so that eventually the child will be able to use it independently.

3. For children who are still small enough for you to lift, we recommend the "human forklift" method. This involves picking the child up, holding him facing away from you, with one arm wrapped around his midsection (pinning his arms if they are flailing or attempting to hit), and the other arm supporting under his legs, so that he is in a semi-sitting position. This method of transporting a child is useful for two reasons: it maintains both your and your child's safety, and it is neither nurturing nor punitive. In this way, you are able to limit the amount of attention to and engagement in the out-of-control behavior, and focus your attention on the problem solving that will occur when the child is calm.

4. If an out-of-control child attempts to hurt you while you are physically assisting him, it is important to give a confident message of parental strength. Calmly saying, "I won't let you hurt me" is more effective than either an angry or pleading, "Don't hit me," because it communicates that you will keep both you and him safe. It is extremely frightening to a child to be allowed to hurt his parent, even though he may try to do so.

The example on page 54 describes how a parent might assist a child to time-out.

Situation: Moira, age 5, and Ben, age 3, playing with new toys
Moira and Ben are excited about the gifts from their
grandmother. Ben becomes interested in Moira's toy and
suddenly grabs it. Moira screams, "Hey, that's mine!"
and begins to hit Ben. Mom steps in to assist.

Mom: [physically pulling Moira away from Ben] "Moira, I
know you're worried about your toy, but I'm afraid Ben is
going to get hurt. Can you take a deep breath and count
to five to calm down?"

Moira: [ignores Mom's coaching, screams, and tries to
pull away from her mother to get to Ben and the toy]

Mom: "I can see that you're really worried! Let's try to
take some deep breaths together." [Mom pulls Moira
close and exaggerates three slow, deep breaths.]

Moira: [continues screaming, attempting to hit both Mom
and Ben]

Mom: [At this point, Mom recognizes that Moira is too
out of control to problem solve. She looks at Ben] "I'm sorry you got hurt. Are you okay?" [she then turns to Moira]
"It looks like you need a few minutes to find your control.
I'll help you." [Mom lifts Moira up, human forklift style,
and begins taking her to her room.]

Moira: "No! No! I'll calm down! I'll calm down! I promise!
I promise!"

Mom: [does not respond verbally; continues to walk
calmly to Moira's room. As she approaches Moira's room,
Moira gets an arm free and slaps Mom in the face. Mom
regains control of Moira's arm.] "I won't let you hurt me.
I'm going to keep both you and me safe." [Mom sets
Moira on the bed, ignores her screaming, and calmly
walks away, shutting the door behind her.]

Later, when Moira is calm, her mother will assist her in
problem solving with Ben as outlined in chapter five.

The example illustrates Moira's mother first attempting to engage Moira in problem solving, then moving to
assisting her to time-out so she can calm down. Despite

Moira's attempts to engage her mother in negotiation and other negative interaction, Moira's mother follows through confidently, and maintains an assertive but neutral stance even when Moira slaps her. (This is not easy to do—breathe deeply and count to yourself!)

While the above example is by no means pretty, we don't want to gloss over the fact that sometimes life with angry kids can get even uglier. In our practice working with parents, many of them report being frustrated that they read parenting books for guidance, they try the skills described, but feel lost again when their experience looks nothing like the pristine examples in the book. Kids may become verbally aggressive, struggle physically on the way into time-out, rush toward the door when you try to leave the room, become destructive in their room during the time-out, or try to get out of the room after you've closed the door.

These are the times when you will have to work the hardest to refrain from returning a child's anger or punishing instead of teaching or coaching. "Practical Questions About Time-Out," Appendix C, offers ideas for handling the often experienced, but least talked about, aspects of time-out for an angry child.

How to hold an out-of-control child. Holding is an alternative to time-out that can have some extra benefits for parents and children. It can be frightening for a child to be out of control. When a parent uses his body to envelop and contain a child, this action can convey a powerful message of support and security, if done in the right spirit. Through your actions you are communicating to your child, "You've lost your control. You're young and haven't had much time to practice self-control. I love you so much that I will lend you my control until you find yours again."

When to use holding
- If you are calm enough to ensure your child's emotional and physical safety

- When your child loses control and there is no safe place available for time-out
- If you feel it is too upsetting for your child to be separated from you when he is out of control
- When your child becomes so out of control in time-out that he hurts himself, others, or property

When not to use holding
- Any time you are feeling frustrated or angry with your child
- When out-of-control behavior seems to be for the purpose of getting attention
- If you feel that you are not physically capable of keeping both you and your child safe

There are several accepted techniques used by counselors for safely holding children, based on the adult's size, the child's size, and the child's behavior. Any time you are considering the possibility of using the holding technique (see illustration), you should first consult a professional to ensure proper technique to avoid injury to yourself or your child.

HANDLING ANGRY BEHAVIOR IN PUBLIC

It is embarrassing and stressful for parents when children have an emotional outburst in public. Such outbursts are particularly difficult because a parent must balance not only the emotional and behavioral needs of his child, but also the rights of others in the environment. If you are not careful, a child can quickly learn that he has the power to manipulate a situation to his benefit by throwing a tantrum in public, since parents may be tempted to give in to avoid an embarrassing scene.

In these situations, your goal is to continue to communicate to your child that his feelings and needs are important, but also to make it clear that others around him have feelings and needs, too. If he is not able to express his feelings in a way that is appropriate to the setting, you should act quickly to help him get to a place where he can calm down. By responding in this way, you give your child three important messages:

- His feelings are important.
- Other people's feelings are also important.
- Limits set in public are as nonnegotiable as they are at home.

Situation: Jared, age 5, and his mother at the grocery store

Lately Jared has had a difficult time dealing with his disappointment when his mother denies requests for treats or toys. Before leaving home for the store, Mom has made sure that Jared had a snack and was well rested.

Mom: "Jared, when we get to the store, we will be shopping for dinner. Today is not a day that we will be choosing any treats or toys. If you see something you want and I say 'no,' you might feel sad or disappointed. Do you have any ideas for how you might help yourself if that happens?"

Jared: "But, Mom, can't I just have a cookie at the bakery?"

Mom: "I can tell you're already thinking about how hard this might be. It's okay for you to be sad, and you can use your words to tell me about how you're feeling if that happens. I'll be there to help you take some deep breaths or give you a hug if you need it."

[Jared and his mother head into the store and finish most of the shopping without incident. When they are nearly done, Jared spots a race car.]

Jared: "Mom, this is the car I've been looking for! Please, Mom, can I have this one just this once?"

Mom: "That is a pretty cool car, buddy. But remember, this is not a trip when we're shopping for toys or treats."

Jared: "But Mommmmmmm . . . "

Mom: "You sound pretty disappointed. I know it's hard when you see something you really want. This would be a great time to take a few deep breaths to help yourself stay calm. Would you like to do that together while we look for the tortillas I need for our taco night?"

Jared: "[now yelling] "Mom—you don't understand! I've been looking for that one my whole life!"

Mom: "Jared, I know this is tough. I can help you find ways to calm down if you need help. If you get so angry and loud that it hurts other people's ears and makes it hard for me to finish our shopping, we will need to leave the store and try again another time."

Jared: "Mom—just shut up. I need that car right now!"

Mom: [takes a deep breath to remain calm] "It looks like this is just too tough right now. I think we'll head home and try another day."

[Mom leaves the store with Jared as calmly as possible, stopping to alert a store employee of her abandoned cart of groceries. At home, she finds some noodles and frozen peas to throw together for dinner. When Jared begins to complain, she resists the temptation to remind him that the lack of groceries is his own "fault," and instead empathizes.]

Mom: "I know this is not what you were hoping to have for dinner. We'll try to get to the store again tomorrow so we can do taco night then."

MANIPULATION BY TANTRUM

In the first two years of life, it is important to respond to children's emotional expressions in order to encourage trust and attachment. While crying can sometimes feel like manipulation in babies and toddlers, it is the only language they have to communicate their feelings and needs and isn't likely to be negative manipulation. However, sometimes older children learn to use the expression of emotion to manipulate adults in inappropriate ways. Most likely you have experienced a time when your child has "turned on" her rage strategically, either to engage you in a negative way or to persuade you to give in on a limit. (In our treatment program, we humorously referred to this as "projectile crying.")

Once you've ruled out that you are not responding from your own level of irritation, trust your instincts regarding whether your child is attempting to manipulate you. If you feel that she is, the best approach is to offer a brief but sincere statement of empathy, followed by a reminder to use her self-soothing or problem-solving skills. At this point, you should exit the scene saying something such as, "If you need some help, you can use your brave words to ask. I'll be in the kitchen." Be sure not to re-engage with your child, either verbally or even with eye contact, as these will likely inadvertently reinforce and extend the length of the tantrum.

SELF-INJURY AS AN EXPRESSION OF ANGER

While many children display aggressive behavior when angry, other children tend to internalize their anger. Children who drive anger inward often injure themselves when they are frustrated or angry. Head banging is particularly common among toddlers, and occasionally for older children. Other forms of self-injury include hitting or pinching themselves, throwing themselves down, or saying self-destructive things.

You can deal with this behavior in the same way you

would if the child were injuring someone else. Focus on setting limits to keep the child safe, rather than engaging in control or punishment. Empathizing, active listening, and helping the child solve the problem are often enough to help the child express her anger more appropriately, instead of turning on herself. When necessary, you can also hold the child and repeat gently, "I can see how frustrated you are. I will help to keep you safe until you feel better." If your child expresses anger by hurting herself over a period of several weeks and you have not been able to redirect her behavior, consult your pediatrician or a child mental health professional for advice on what to do next.

In chapter four, we have covered ways to stay calm under stress and how to calm an already angry child, keeping everyone safe in the process. In chapter five, you will learn how to help your child take the next steps toward problem solving.

POINTS TO REMEMBER

- Very young children can learn simple tools to manage their anger.
- Teach (before you need it) and coach (in the moment) children in the use of anger management tools.
- Time-out, *when used positively,* can become a calming tool children will eventually use independently.
- For the extremely out-of-control child, set limits for safety, rather than trying to control or punish the child.

5

Tools Kids Need to Solve
Individual and Social Problems

We hope chapter four made a good case for the importance of helping your child become calm before attempting to deal with a problem. The next step is to assist her in the development of problem-solving skills. The good news is that when she can approach a troubling situation equipped with good problem-solving strategies, *she will be less likely to become angry in the first place.* We will talk about two categories of problems: individual and social problems. The first involves only the child, the second, her larger world of siblings and parents, playmates and classmates.

INDIVIDUAL PROBLEM SOLVING

Individual problems are those a child encounters that do not involve another person. Often these problems are associated with completing a task or learning a new skill. Examples of such situations are trying to tie a shoe, learning a new sport, or doing homework or chores.

A parent's role in helping a child learn to solve problems depends on the child's age, maturity, and experience in problem solving. The developmental guidelines in Appendix A can assist you in determining how much support your child needs as she learns problem-solving skills. Below are the steps for problem solving.

Steps to Parent-Guided Individual Problem Solving

1. *Listen actively for feelings and label them.*
   Stop what you're doing, get down on your child's eye level, and ensure that your face and voice convey empathy. Even if your child isn't yet using feelings words, figure out and label the most likely primary feeling your child is experiencing.

2. *Reflect feelings and connect them to the situation.*
   "It looks like you're frustrated because . . . "

3. *Look for alternatives and evaluate the consequences of each one.*
   Help your child brainstorm several possible solutions. Resist the temptation to veto "bad" ideas. Then help your child evaluate each alternative by using the three Rs:
   • Respectful: "Is it fair? How might other people feel?"
   • Reasonable: "Is it safe? Could it work?"
   • Rules: "Does it break any rules?"

When you consistently use each of these steps with your child from an early age, it gives your child the familiarity, experience, and practice she needs for this complex set of skills to become more natural and intuitive. Practice is especially important because when your child needs the skills is the exact time she will be least able to access them. Each time you model or practice these skills with your child, it's "money in the bank" for her to eventually use the skills on her own. Consider the following examples, each describing a child at a different developmental or experience level, and the parents' responses.

Situation: Jeremy, age 9 months, wants his toy dog

Jeremy has recently begun to crawl. He sees his favorite stuffed dog across the room, but is frustrated that he cannot reach it. He begins to fuss. Mom notices the fussing, and lies down alongside Jeremy.

Mom: [makes eye contact, and shows an empathetic face] (Listen actively for feelings)

Mom: "Oh, you sound frustrated. You want to get to your dog, but it's hard!" (Reflect feelings and connect them to the situation) "What should we do? I could move it closer, I could let you use me to push against so you could get there by yourself, I could distract you or comfort you. I think moving it closer might be good, because you really want to get it yourself!" (Look for alternatives and evaluate consequences)

[Mom pushes the dog closer, and Jeremy crawls the shorter distance to get to it, smiling and cooing. Mom claps her hands enthusiastically.]

Mom: "Yeah, that worked. You did it!" (Choose a solution and follow up)

While Mom does most of the work, she recognizes the value in having worked through the steps out loud, both for her own practice as well as Jeremy's benefit. While you may feel silly problem solving out loud for an infant, babies are constantly learning from our language, facial expressions, and voice tones. Many experts believe that if you take what you think your baby understands and double it, you will be about right.

Situation: Gretchen, age 4, looking for her favorite doll

Mom notices Gretchen beginning to cry as she frantically

rummages through her toy box. She kneels down beside her, showing concern.

Mom: "What's the matter, honey?" (Listen actively for feelings)

Gretchen: "I can't find Tabitha!"

Mom: "Are you worried because you can't find your favorite dolly?" (Reflect feelings and connect them to the situation)

Gretchen: "Yeah! I need her!"

Mom: "Hmmm . . . you look pretty sad and frustrated." (More reflection of feelings) "Let's take three deep breaths before we decide what to do."

Gretchen: "I think Julie took it! Let's look in her room!"

Mom: "Well, you could do that. How do you think Julie might feel if we looked through her things while she's not home?" (Look for alternatives and evaluate consequences)

Gretchen: "Mad, I guess—but I need Tabitha!"

Mom: "So should we look for Tabitha in the playroom, or should we find a different toy until Julie gets home?"

Gretchen: "Let's look in the playroom." (Look for alternatives and evaluate consequences) "Can you help me?"

Mom: "Sure. You're a good problem-solver!"

Whether the doll is found or not, this experience has been a good exercise for Gretchen. If they find the doll, Mom will follow up to point out that the problem solving worked. If they do not, Mom will help Gretchen re-evaluate and try another solution. (Follow up)

As you can see, this example demonstrates the ways that Mom offers suggestions and support for problem solving in her role as teacher. She balances the delicate interplay between teaching and taking action. Mom recognizes that while she wants to teach Gretchen about her choices and their consequences in this situation, she also needs to keep the momentum moving toward resolution.

This allows Gretchen to do some age-appropriate learning without overwhelming her frustration tolerance.

Situation: Jason, age 9, having trouble with baseball

Jason has struck out every time he has been at bat in his past two Little League games. He gets into the car, slamming the door.

Jason: "I hate baseball, I stink, I'm the worst player in the universe!"

Dad: "You sound pretty frustrated about your hitting slump." (Listen actively for feelings)

Jason: "It's not a slump, I'm just terrible."

Dad: "I can tell it's really got you down, buddy." (Listen actively for feelings)

Jason: "I'm never going to get a hit again."

Dad: "I'm sure it feels like that. Can you think of any ways you might solve the problem you're having with hitting?" (Look for alternatives)

Jason: "I'm just going to quit the team!"

Dad: "I think it's hard to think about different solutions when you're still feeling so frustrated. Let's talk about this more after dinner."

Jason: "Mmm."

At this point, Dad realizes that Jason is not ready to problem solve, and he chooses to stay focused on active listening and empathizing with Jason's feelings. Often when a child is very upset, he may not be immediately ready to move into problem solving, and if given empathy and some time, he will be willing to problem solve later.

After dinner . . .

Dad: [goes into Jason's room, and sits on his bed with him] "Hey, buddy, how are you doing?"

Jason: [still somewhat sullen] "Fine."

Dad: "Before dinner, you were thinking you might solve

your hitting problem by quitting the team. I was thinking how in our family we make sure we solve problems by using the three Rs—we try to be respectful, reasonable, and follow the rules. How do you think your coach might feel if he suddenly didn't have his right fielder on the team?" (Evaluate consequences)

Jason: "Well, bad, I guess."

Dad: "Yeah, you're right. Your coach would probably be disappointed. You made a commitment, and I know he's counting on you." [Dad takes an opportunity to translate "bad" into "disappointed," modeling primary feelings and helping Jason have empathy for his coach.]

Jason: "I just wish I could hit like the other kids."

Dad: "Well, what do you think we could do to help you out?" (Look for alternatives and evaluate consequences)

Jason: "I don't know. Maybe I just need more practice. Or maybe I'm getting too stressed out about hitting, and psyching myself out, like you say sometimes the major leaguers do."

Dad: "Well, those both seem like solvable problems to me. What do you think?"

Jason: [brightening up] "Do you think we could go to the batting cages a few times this week to practice?"

Dad: "Sure—that's a great idea. Let's do that Wednesday when I get home from work, and Saturday morning, okay?"

Jason: "Thanks, Dad."

Dad: "Now, what about this 'psyching yourself out' thing?" (Look for alternatives and evaluate consequences)

Jason: "Well, maybe I need to do some of that stuff you always talk about, like picturing myself hitting the ball before I get up to bat, and telling myself positive things as I'm batting."

Dad: "Those are great ideas, buddy. And remember, major leaguers only hit about 3 out of 10 times, even when they are doing great. You've got to take it easy on yourself. These things take time. Let's see how things go for your next game, and we can talk again afterward to see how your plan is working." (Follow up)

The first key to Dad's success is that he empathized with Jason's feelings. He also gave him time to calm down when he realized Jason wasn't ready to problem solve. Dad might have been tempted to give Jason a lecture about responsibility and commitment. However, he wisely chose to allow Jason to deal with his feelings, and then used a supportive line of questioning, including some discussion of family values and the "three Rs" to help Jason reach his own conclusion about quitting. If Dad had chosen to confront Jason when he was still upset, Jason probably would have stuck to his decision to quit. He may never have been able to do any problem solving.

You can see that Dad has taught Jason about problem solving, empathy, and their family values (the three Rs) in neutral times. After Jason calmed down, he was able to take part in the problem solving.

Once Dad had empathized and coached Jason through the problem-solving steps, he then offered Jason encouragement and extra information by reminding him about how even major league baseball players strike out. Dad's timing here was important. If Dad had started by trying to reassure Jason, he might have inadvertently undermined the problem-solving process. As parents, we all feel the desire to "make it better" for our kids when they are in pain, by offering reassurance and/or correction of their misconceptions. The problem with this is that when we don't allow them to process their feelings, they may feel unheard. Giving them the support they need to talk their feelings through and work toward a solution helps them to gain the experience and confidence they need to tackle problems in the future.

Situation: Alexandra, age 12, working on her science project

Dad hears Alexandra call out in anger. He comes in to see what is happening.

Dad: "You sound upset. What's happening?" (Listen actively for feelings)

Alexandra: "The stupid cat knocked over part of my project, and I don't have any of the materials left to re-do it."

Dad: "Oh man, that's disappointing. I know how hard you've been working on it." (Reflect feelings and connect them to the situation)

Alexandra: "Ugh, that cat makes me crazy!"

Dad: "Do you feel like you want some help, or do you think you're okay?"

Alexandra: "I don't know yet; I've got to figure out what I'm going to do." (Look for alternatives and evaluate consequences)

Dad: "Okay—I'll be in the kitchen working on the dishes. If you need anything, let me know."

[Dad leaves; 15 minutes pass]

Alexandra: "Dad, I think I know how to fix my project, but I need some more toothpicks and glue. I know it's late, but this is due tomorrow. Can you take me to get those tonight?" (Choose a solution)

This example shows a child who has had plenty of exposure to and experience in problem solving. Her dad still offers empathy and support, but knows that Alexandra has the confidence and skills to solve her problem. He leaves her with a reminder that he is there if she needs him, and when she has worked out a solution, he is happy to provide the physical assistance she needs.

Remember the teaching role you take as a parent depends both on the child's age as well as her experience with problem solving. A twelve-year-old with more limited exposure to using healthy problem-solving skills would have needed her parent to be a comforter as well as a teacher. However, a child as young as seven years old, who had been exposed to positive problem solving throughout her life, might have been ready for a parent to function more as a coach.

SOCIAL PROBLEM SOLVING

Social problem solving is more complex because children must deal with a problem and also the interests and feelings of another person. In order to be successful, children will still need the skills to process feelings and use the problem-solving steps you saw in action in the previous examples. However, they need to add negotiation skills and a greater capacity to empathize with others in order to resolve social conflicts.

As with personal problem solving, a parent's role depends on the child's development and experience using the skills. However, an added problem for the parent in social situations is the tendency to take over for kids. Traditionally, parents have seen their job as judge and jury, deciding who is right and wrong, and doling out rewards and punishments accordingly. If the goal of parenting is to help kids function independently someday, then given the choice between controlling and teaching, we want to choose teaching as often as possible.

As the table on page 70 shows, a parent who is judge increases the potential for sibling rivalry by setting up the appearance of a parent choosing one child over another. Over time, this can lead one child to become the "good child" and the other, the troublemaker. In contrast, parent-guided problem solving helps to build children's skills, confidence, self-esteem, and relationships with others. When you remove yourself from the role of judge, parenting is much more pleasurable and rewarding. Instead of being the bad guy, you can be a supporter and resource to your children.

Situation: Parent as judge

Brianna, age 5, and her brother, Dylan, age 7, are playing in the living room. Mom hears Brianna shriek, "Stop that!" and begin to cry. Mom quickly enters the room to deal with the situation.

Mom: "Dylan, what did you do now?"

Parent as Judge

Parent's Actions	What the Child Learns
Immediately takes control of the situation	When there is a problem, the best solution is to yell for an adult, or tattle
Decides who is right, who is wrong	Problems can only be solved with adult intervention
Decides solution and/or punishment; lectures and scolds	When adults help solve the problem, kids "win" or "lose"

Parent as Conflict Manager

Parent's Actions	What the Child Learns
Ensures safety by helping kids calm down	Adults provide structure, safety, and guidance when there is a conflict
Takes on role as facilitator	Kids are capable of finding solutions to problems
Uses guided discussion to help each child verbalize his/her point of view	Problems can often be solved fairly for all
Guides brainstorming solutions, within family rules and values	If a child needs help to solve a problem, adults will listen to his/her point of view and feelings, and will help think of possible solutions
Remains neutral, allowing kids to reach a decision acceptable to both/all	Having a problem doesn't mean someone gets into trouble. There are mutually beneficial solutions.

Brianna: "He took the Lego I was going to use, and when I took it back he hit me!"

Dylan: "I did not! It was sitting right there, you weren't even touching it!"

Mom: [taking the Lego from Dylan and handing it to Brianna] "Dylan, you are the oldest. You know better. And if you two can't play nicely, I'm going to put the Legos away."

Situation: Parent as conflict manager

Mom: "It sounds like you two have a problem. I'm going

to give each of you a chance to say what you think happened. We'll start with Brianna."

Brianna: "He took the Lego I was going to use, and when I took it back he hit . . . "

Dylan: [interrupting] "I did not!"

Mom: "Dylan, remember you will have a chance to talk in a minute. Right now it's Brianna's turn. So, Brianna, there was a Lego you were planning to use, and when Dylan picked it up you took it back?"

Brianna: "Yeah. And then he hit me!"

Mom: "So how are you feeling about what happened?"

Brianna: "I was really mad that he took my Lego, because he knew I was going to use it next."

Mom: "All right, so you were mad and maybe a little disappointed that Dylan used the Lego you were hoping to use?"

Brianna: "Yes."

Mom: "Okay. So, Dylan, tell me what you remember happening?"

Dylan: "She didn't even have the Lego in her hand, so I picked it up to use, and then she just grabbed it out of my hand."

Mom: "And what happened next?"

Dylan: "Well, I was really mad at her for taking the Lego, so I hit her. But not that hard!"

Brianna: [interrupting] "Yuh huh! It hurt a lot! See the mark?"

Mom: "Brianna, I know you're upset, but it's Dylan's turn to talk right now. So, Dylan, how are you feeling about what happened?"

Dylan: "Well, I was mad that she snatched the Lego from me. How was I supposed to know she wanted to use it?"

Mom: "Okay, so you were probably surprised that she took the Lego out of your hand, and also mad about it. You've both done a nice job of talking about the problem and listening to each other's feelings. Brianna, what is one thing you think you could do to solve this problem?"

Brianna: "Well, I could tell Dylan next time which Legos I'm gonna need to build my house."

Mom: "And if Dylan accidentally takes one you think you need, can you think of a better way to let him know?"
Brianna: "I could use my words and ask for it."
Mom: "Those sound like good ideas. Dylan, how would you handle things differently next time?"
Dylan: "I guess I should have used my words when she grabbed it from me, instead of hitting her."
Mom: "You've both come up with some really great ideas that will help you have a happier time playing together. I know that you'll be able to use some of these good ideas to solve the problem next time."

If your child is struggling with anger and problem solving, you may find the above example unrealistic. And the truth is, if you have just begun to introduce this style of problem solving to your child, it would be unrealistic to expect this result! It takes dozens and dozens of opportunities for kids to practice the skills to become even minimally proficient in this kind of problem solving, not to mention to build their trust in the process.

It can be extremely frustrating in the initial stages for parents to invest the amount of time and energy it takes to model and teach these skills. You may even be tempted to give up after five, six, or thirty attempts. But we can assure you that our experiences with children, parents, and in classrooms tell us that kids are capable of engaging successfully in this kind of facilitated problem solving. And believe it or not, they will eventually even shock you by beginning to do it independently! If starting this seems daunting or you're unsure how to proceed, consult Appendix D for "Getting Started with Conflict Management," where you will find common questions answered.

Five Steps to Conflict Management

1. Give all children a turn to tell their version of what happened without interruption or correction from anyone.

2. Ask all children how they felt about what happened.

3. Ask all children to give suggestions for what they could do to solve the problem.

4. Assist children to choose solutions they feel are *respectful, reasonable,* and within family *rules* and values.

5. Help children evaluate the success of their chosen solution, and to choose another if needed.

There is considerable crossover between the skills children need to be successful solving individual problems and doing so with social problems—the skills learned in one category help in the other. Modeling, teaching, and practicing these skills may seem labor intensive at first. (They are!) However, parents who stick with it will see positive results in family and peer relationships, as well as school performance. And the benefits for skillful problem solvers reach far beyond home and school, into adult relationships, marital satisfaction, and career success.

In chapter five, you have learned ways to help your child solve problems. In chapter six, we will discuss how to help kids handle life's unsolvable problems.

POINTS TO REMEMBER

- Children's personal and social problems provide powerful opportunities to teach and coach.
- Remember the importance of genuine active listening *before* helping children problem solve.
- Encourage children to use the three Rs as their guideline for evaluating possible solutions.
- Parents are most effective as conflict managers, rather than judges.

6

Tools Kids Need to Deal with Problems Outside Their Control

Not every problem can be solved in the ways introduced in chapters four and five. There are two kinds of unsolvable problems for children: when a parent sets a nonnegotiable limit and when life circumstances create situations that are outside the child's control.

Every unsolvable problem bears the theme of loss and grieving, no matter how big or small the issue. Understanding this can help parents feel more confident and empathetic as they attempt to help their children deal with the realities of life. Below are examples of unsolvable problems.

Nonnegotiable parental limits
- Mom says "no" to a television show
- Dad denies a request for candy before dinner
- Bedtime can't be rescheduled

- Mom doesn't allow a friend to spend the night
- Dad says video game time is over
- Mom says that clothing is inappropriate

Life circumstances
- A friend moves away
- The family moves and the child must change schools
- A parent returns to work
- Parents get divorced
- A child goes into foster care
- A child develops a serious illness
- Someone in the family dies

NONNEGOTIABLE PARENTAL LIMITS

Nonnegotiable parental limits, while frustrating for children, are an important and unavoidable part of healthy child development. *We can't, and shouldn't try, to shield children from dealing with the feelings resulting from having appropriate limits set.* Each time you set a limit for your child, you are not only teaching him about safety and family values, you are also giving him the opportunity to practice the skills from chapter four for managing intense feelings. Each time he practices these skills he becomes better prepared for when life's larger losses inevitably occur. A parent's role in these situations is not to solve the problem or rescue a child from his feelings, but rather to support the child while he experiences and deals with them.

Despite your best intentions, you may find your child's strong emotions bring out even stronger feelings in you. Our responses to our children at these times are influenced by present and past experiences. Perhaps your own parents were uncomfortable with strong feelings and responded by punishing you, ignoring your feelings, or even giving in to your pleas. Or in the moment you're attempting to set a limit for your child, you happen to be frustrated with your spouse, worried about finances, and exhausted from the day-to-day demands of being a parent. Chapter seven discusses these issues in depth, but for now just being aware of your tendencies to either give in or get angry when your child is angry can help you begin to adjust your responses.

The following example illustrates the different outcomes for a parent who is attempting to use positive skills with her child. In the first example, she allows her frustration to get the better of her, pushing her to old ways of responding. In the second, she uses anger management strategies and has a more successful outcome.

Situation: Andrew, age 7, playing a video game

Roxanne is a committed and caring mother who has worked very hard to give her children a more stable home life than she experienced. She grew up in a family with an alcoholic father and an anxious, passive mother. When there was conflict, her father often became explosive and enraged, while her mother attempted to keep the peace and the children safe by staying out of his way. Often she would accomplish this by bribing the children or giving in on limits so they would not feel bad or express their feelings, potentially enraging their father even more.

Yesterday, Roxanne and her husband had an argument about their strained financial situation. She did not sleep well, as a result, and is feeling irritable and tired today. Her son Andrew is playing his video game. The family rule is that Andrew can play up to one hour of video games per day, and his daily time is nearly up. Roxanne lets him know that he has five more minutes to play. When his time is up, she asks him to turn off the game. Andrew first ignores her, then asks for more time, and ultimately becomes angry when she enforces the original limit.

Giving in to old habit
Roxanne: "I know it's hard to stop in the middle of a level, but one hour of video game time is our rule."
Andrew: "But, Mom, I worked forever to get to level 5. I'll never get that far again!"

Roxanne: "I can see how frustrating and disappointing that is."

Andrew: "Stop talking, you're making me mess up!"

Roxanne: [beginning to get frustrated] "Andrew, turn the game off. Now."

Andrew: [yelling] "You are so mean! All my friends get to play as much as they want. I hate you!" [throws the controller at her]

Roxanne: "That's it! I am sick and tired of your mouth. I will not be treated this way!" [grabs the video game] "This thing is going in the garbage!"

Andrew: [screaming] "I hate you, I hate you, I hate you!" [begins hitting at her]

Roxanne roughly grabs Andrew, takes him to his room, and shoves him to his bed, slamming the door as she leaves. As she begins to calm down, she thinks, "Man, I really blew that. I acted just like my dad used to. Ugh, I'm a terrible mother."

Roxanne: [returning to Andrew's room] "Honey, I'm really sorry I got so angry. If you want to, you can play an extra 30 minutes of video games while I finish up with dinner."

New way, using anger management skills

Roxanne: "I know it's hard to stop in the middle of a level, but one hour of video game time is our rule."

Andrew: "But, Mom, I worked forever to get to level 5. I'll never get that far again!"

Roxanne: "I can see how frustrating and disappointing that is."

Andrew: "Stop talking, you're making me mess up!"

Roxanne: [beginning to get frustrated] "Andrew, it's time to turn off the game. I'm going to the bathroom, and you can either turn it off by yourself while I'm gone, or I'll do it when I get back." [Roxanne goes to the bathroom as a way to take an *adult time-out,* sensing that she is becoming too frustrated to handle the situation calmly. She spends two minutes in the bathroom breathing deeply, using positive self-talk to encourage herself, and visualizing how she wants to handle the situation. When she returns to Andrew, he is still playing the game.]

Andrew: "No, no, Mom, just a minute, just a minute . . . "
[Roxanne calmly walks over and turns off the game]

Andrew: [yelling] "You are so mean! All my friends get to play as much as they want. I hate you!" [throws the controller at her]

Roxanne: [calmly assists him to his room] "It's okay to be frustrated and angry, and it's not okay to hurt me. You can take a few minutes to calm down in your room."

After a few minutes, Roxanne goes back to Andrew's room and discusses what happened. As a part of the discussion, Roxanne explains that she feels playing the video game is too intense for Andrew right now, and that this week she will help him find some calmer things to do and she will help him practice ways to handle disappointment and frustration. Next week he can try again.

The key difference between the two scenes is Roxanne's awareness of her own frustration level. In the first example, Roxanne does not attend to her growing frustration, and when Andrew becomes verbally and physically aggressive, she follows her father's example from her own childhood. After she blows up, she is able to calm down and think about her response, and feelings of guilt and shame creep in. Roxanne does not want to parent in the same ways her father did, and now finds herself desperately wanting to repair the damage. Unfortunately, Roxanne's model for repair is her mother, who tended to give in on limits to keep the peace. By not managing her own anger and frustration, Roxanne is inadvertently both aggressive and permissive, rather than assertive with Andrew. Each time she allows herself to respond in this way, she reinforces the pattern, both in her own behavior and in Andrew's development of negative behavior toward others and poor coping skills.

In the second scene, Roxanne manages her strong emotions, so that she is able to react in a calm, assertive way. She recognizes that it is perfectly normal for a child to manage anger poorly at times. In fact, since she expects this to be part of Andrew's learning process, she is much less likely to become angry herself. Roxanne understands that it is not her role to get between Andrew and his feelings by either responding with her own anger or by rescuing him from his feelings. Instead, she calmly offers both empathy and structure by setting immediate limits to his aggression. She also follows up with a longer-term logical consequence to help him learn better coping skills that reflect family rules and values.

NATURAL AND LOGICAL CONSEQUENCES

A powerful part of managing your own emotions with your children is feeling confident in using natural and logical consequences to set limits. Typically, traditional punishment is not connected to what the child did, is delivered in an angry or hostile tone, and feels to the child like the adult is attempting to get even or retaliate. This damages the relationship over time. Natural and logical consequences, however, fall into the realm of discipline. They are different from traditional punishment in that they are logically related to what the child did and, while firm, are delivered in the spirit of teaching and limiting behavior, rather than punishing.

Natural consequences

Natural consequences are those that occur naturally without any parental intervention. Natural consequences are good teachers and keep the parent out of the middle, since the environment or situation is delivering the consequence. Parents can spend their energy empathizing and problem solving, rather than lecturing or punishing.

Example
- Drake leaves his toy outside, and it is ruined in the rain. His father empathizes with his sadness and helps problem solve. Together they think of what Drake can do to earn money to replace the toy. Dad avoids saying, "I told

you that's what would happen if you weren't responsible,"
and does not shield Drake from experiencing the consequence of his own behavior by buying him another toy.
Note: Sometimes natural consequences are too dangerous
to let a child experience or too far in the future for the child
to learn anything. Some situations have no natural consequence. In these situations, a parent can use a logical consequence.

Logical consequences

Logical consequences are consequences that a parent provides in a firm and friendly manner. They are connected to
what the child did and intended to teach what happens
when a child violates social values and standards.

Examples
- Liam refuses to put away his toys. Mom puts them up for
  a day (or week, depending on age).
- Jennifer kicks a hole in the wall when she's angry. Dad
  has her use her allowance money to help pay for repair
  and requires her to help fix the hole.
- Charity scratches her friend Stephanie's arm when she
  strikes out in anger. After a time-out to calm down, Mom
  has Charity rub some aloe vera on the scratch and check
  to see if there is any other way she can help Stephanie
  feel better.

Consequences should be related to what the child did, be
reasonable, and be delivered respectfully. If you are accustomed to using punishment, it may be challenging to find
consequences that are logically related to a particular situation, but this gets easier as you practice. Give yourself a
few minutes to decide on the consequence.

LIFE CIRCUMSTANCES

Events such as moves, divorce, and death are often unavoidable. These events are traumatic enough for adults,

who may have at least some level of control in the situation. For children, these events can be devastating. They have no control over the situation. They have fewer resources with which to cope and their ability to understand what is going on is less developed than an adult's. They cannot express emotions verbally very well. Finally they have limited life experience from which they can draw the hope that things will get better. Given all these limitations, children really need a parent's help!

In traumatic situations, it is important for parents to support and guide children in expressing their feelings and grieving. Most loving parents want to shield a child from pain, so we may look for ways to "make it stop." The table below lists the common mistakes parents make when trying to help their children manage grief.

Common Mistakes in Handling Grief

Mistake		Example
Minimizing:	Downplaying the severity of the problem	A child's best friend moves away: "Oh, honey, don't worry. You'll make another friend."
Rescuing:	Offering ways for the child to avoid his/her feelings through distraction or overindulgence	A child has to change schools: "Don't be sad. Let's get you some new school clothes."
Shaming:	Communicating that his/her feelings are not acceptable	A pet dies: "You've cried long enough. It's just a cat."
Projecting:	Expecting the child to feel and express the same intensity of emotion as the adult	A grandparent dies: "How can you play at a time like this?"
Role reversal:	Asking the child to take care of the adult	Parents are divorcing: "I don't know how I'm going to get through this. Come here, darling. Give Mommy a hug."

How children experience grief

Swiss psychiatrist Elisabeth Kubler-Ross developed a widely accepted five-stage model for understanding the stages of grief. Knowing the stages of grief will help you understand your child's responses. The stages are: denial, anger, bargaining, depression, and acceptance. Though every person moves through the stages in different ways, in most cases all of the stages are visited. Some people stay longer in one stage than another, or come back and revisit some of the stages throughout the course of grieving. When a person is allowed to grieve in a healthy way, he will eventually reach the final stage of acceptance. Children move through these stages just as adults do, though children behave differently from adults.

Five Stages of Grief

1. Denial: Children may experience numbness, avoidance, isolation, or direct denial.

2. Anger: Once past denial, children will be angry about the loss and may act out or take out their anger on other people or things around them.

3. Bargaining: Children look for ways to get back what was lost, or find someone or something to blame (including themselves).

4. Depression: This is a time of sadness in which children may feel helpless or hopeless and express sadness through crying or withdrawal.

5. Acceptance: Though still sad, children begin to reorganize their thinking to include the loss.

Children's behavior in grieving

During denial, children's emotional response may seem dull, or unusual for the situation. Child may ask for or seek out the person who has died. Child may fantasize that the divorcing parents are still together or may reunite. Children may refuse to discuss the loss, deny any feelings at all, or lose themselves in an activity for long periods.

In the anger stage, children may verbalize their anger and also act out physically toward people, animals, or objects. They may express extreme anger at seemingly insignificant things.

When bargaining, children may say, "If I promise to be good, will Daddy come back?" Children may also blame others for their loss: "Why did you have to be so mean to Mommy and make her leave?"

In the depression stage, children may be tearful, irritable, lethargic, or withdrawn. Their sleep or appetite may be affected. They may lose interest in favorite activities. They may isolate themselves from family and friends.

Finally, in accepting loss, children return to life as usual. They may be more able to talk about their loss and to integrate it into their life story. They may revisit major losses as they develop and can understand the loss in new ways.

Remember that grief has its own timetable. We tend to give children support in the initial stages and forget that grieving takes a long time. When it resurfaces as anger at a later developmental stage, it is important to remember the connection to the original trauma.

Divorce, in particular, elicits periodic anger in children, partially because of the ongoing nature of the loss. Consider the following story illustrating the connection between grief and angry behavior.

Situation: Cindy, age 7, whose parents are divorced

Cindy's parents divorced when she was four years old. She remained with her mother, Julia, and visited her father every other weekend. Both parents understood that these changes would be very upsetting to Cindy, and they supported her through her confusion, sadness, and anger. For a while, Cindy wet the bed at night, threw more tantrums, and was more aggressive. Since both parents expected this and saw it as a normal response, they handled it with empathy, patience, and consistency.

Three years later, Cindy suddenly became more irritable, sullen, and defiant. Her mother noticed that she had started talking back and fighting about chores. Though Julia tried to remain calm, she became increasingly frustrated by Cindy's behavior. After a particularly trying afternoon, Cindy refused to help clear the table after dinner. Julia angrily sent Cindy to her room. As she stomped off, Cindy yelled, "You're mean. No wonder Daddy left!"

Once Julia calmed down after this volley, she realized that Cindy's recent uncooperative behavior was related to her anger and grief regarding the divorce. She gave Cindy some time to calm down, and then sat down to talk. Cindy shared that several weeks ago during a class project on family trees, she was embarrassed that she was the only child in her group who had divorced parents. Cindy described feeling sad and angry. Julia reassured Cindy that all of her feelings were okay and encouraged her to continue talking about them, so they would be less likely to come out in her behavior. Julia recognized that this will likely be the first of many times throughout Cindy's childhood that they will need to deal with the ways the divorce has impacted Cindy's life.

We often forget to stop and see a loss through the child's eyes. Sometimes it happens because we are caught up in our own grieving, and possibly are in a different stage of grief than our child. Or we may just be too overwhelmed ourselves and cannot comprehend the magnitude of our child's emotional reaction to trauma.

An example of extreme trauma is when children are placed into foster care. While professionals and foster parents understand this is very difficult for children, we nevertheless often expect them to adapt much more quickly than is realistic. We hope they will be able to verbalize their anger and sadness, and when they express it behaviorally (which is much more likely), we lose patience. In the spirit of seeing this kind of loss through a child's eyes, consider the following hypothetical example.

Imagine that when you arrive home from work today, a stranger greets you at the door. She explains that she is a social worker, here to take you to your new family, because she is worried that you are not safe here. Despite your protests that your spouse is kind and your children are wonderful, she insists that you go with her. A police officer restrains your crying spouse and children, while you are assisted to the car, carrying a garbage bag of a few belongings selected for you. You arrive at a new, unfamiliar home, and are introduced to your new spouse and children. The social worker explains that she's not sure when you will be able to see your "old" family again, but that this new family will love you and take care of you. Within a few weeks, you are expected to behave as a member of this family in all ways. Of course, this means you will be intimate with your new spouse and will provide consistent and loving care to your new children.

If you can truly empathize with this imaginary *you*, what emotions might you be feeling? What extreme behaviors might you show as a result of those feelings? What do you feel would be a legitimate time line for you to work through the stages of grief? Now imagine all of these same feelings and behaviors through the eyes of a person who has the life experience and coping skills of a five-year-old or a ten-year-old. And what if this wasn't the first time this had happened, and you had experienced many other losses and traumas in addition to this one?

Certainly, there are many complicated reasons that children enter the foster care system, and this example is not a criticism of foster care. Our intent is to allow you to experience in your imagination an extremely traumatic experience from a child's perspective. Empathizing allows us to understand more fully why a child may be angry, and helps us have realistic expectations for the child's grieving. When you can look at any experience from the child's point of view, you will feel compelled to find ways to support such a child's grieving in healthy ways, rather than becoming a participant in his or her sometimes upsetting, angry behavior.

There are many resources to guide parents in helping children cope with grief and loss. If you feel that you have a child who is struggling with grief, please see Recommended Reading at the end of the book for additional resources.

In chapter six, we have discussed how to help kids handle life's unsolvable problems. In chapter seven, we will talk about ways you can manage your own anger in order to be the best possible support to your child.

POINTS TO REMEMBER

- Allow children to feel their emotions resulting from unsolvable problems.
- Support and empathize with children while they deal with their feelings.
- Avoid minimizing, rescuing, shaming, projecting, or role reversal when helping children with grief.

Tools Parents Need to Take Care of Their Own Intense Feelings

One of the most difficult aspects of being a parent is remaining calm while dealing with an out-of-control child. On any given day, a parent deals with exhaustion, stress, and outside pressures, not to mention the many basic tasks required to keep a household running. Add to all of this an angry child who is having tantrums, and may even be verbally and physically aggressive, and it is no wonder we all sometimes feel like we are losing it. Make no mistake—this is hard work!

The most important thing you can do to raise a child who manages anger in healthy ways is to learn to do so yourself. Children observe their parents closely: what they model in handling their own anger is the most powerful teacher.

A parent who models good anger management in the process of assisting an angry child makes a huge positive impact. Picture the difference between a parent who routinely gets bigger and angrier when a child is angry, and a parent who remains calm and offers emotional support while limiting inappropriate behavior. In the first situation, a child learns that his parent's feelings always dominate his own, leading to a breakdown in the relationship. In the other, a child learns he has a supportive mentor whom he can trust.

This chapter will help you figure out why you might be angry at times. It gives you the tools you need to manage your feelings so that you can be the positive example you want to be for your children.

VALUES: THEIR IMPACT ON ANGER

Values are the standards of behavior that guide our lives. While cultures hold certain values in common, among individuals there may be a broad range in what each considers important. Without communication between parenting partners, conflicting values can create serious problems.

Prioritizing your values—deciding which are the most important to you—has a practical benefit. It allows you to make day-to-day choices that reflect what is important to you. For example, one of your personal values may be cleanliness, while another may be allowing your child to explore his environment. You can see immediately how these two values could be in conflict when your curious child wishes to find out what's under the log in the muddy garden. Which one will be your priority? On a daily basis, you may have to make quick decisions about which value will take precedence. You may find your decision driven by your energy level or mood more than by your core beliefs. Often the stress from values conflicts produces unexpected anger, leaving you feeling guilty later and wondering why you "lost it." The following activity shows a list of values that many of us hold. This exercise will help you prioritize some of your values.

Exercise: Prioritizing Parental Values

Think of some of the values you wish to instill in your children. Put a number 1 by those on the list that are the most important, 2 by those moderately important, and 3 by those least important. Add other values you hold.

_1_ independent   _3_ creative

_3_ compliant/obedient   _2_ strong-minded

_1_ honest   _2_ adaptable

_2_ polite   _1_ persevering

_1_ caring   _1_ flexible

_2_ competitive   ___ _____

_2_ assertive   ___ _____

_1_ respectful   ___ _____

_3_ neat   ___ _____

Now look at all the items you marked with a one. Are there potential conflicts among them? For example, you may have chosen both independent and compliant, caring and honest, and neat and creative. This is not to say that you can't have a child who is both independent and compliant, kind and honest, or neat and creative. However, you must be aware of your values so that in the moment of decision you are able to prioritize based on the greater good.

For example, when your four-year-old is getting a bit overzealous with a painting project, rather than have a knee-jerk angry reaction because of the mess, you can decide if this is a moment when creativity supercedes neatness. Often you can find a way to satisfy both values (for example, putting newspaper down under your little painter), but you must remain calm to make the best decision in the moment.

The values listed in the exercise are but a few of the many you might wish for your children. You can prioritize the values *you* live by, too, to make sure that how you spend *your time* reflects those most important to you. Everyday we have to make hard choices about what we can and can't do: choices about how much and where we will work, which hobbies we will pursue, which outside activities our kids are involved in, and whether we agree to bake cookies for the PTA bake sale, build props for the school play, or coach a team.

The key is to make sure your decisions about how you spend your time are purposeful and value driven, and that you recognize that sometimes you have to say "no," even to worthwhile endeavors. This kind of purposefulness can go a long way in reducing anger.

REALISTIC EXPECTATIONS

Another way to reduce the possibility of anger is to have realistic expectations of yourself and your child. Expecting perfection from either of you sets an unreasonable standard. You both may end up feeling hopeless and angry. Remember to "Aim high and forgive yourself a dozen times a day." Remain committed to your values, and be kind to yourself and your child as you grow.

HOW DO YOU EXPRESS ANGER?

All of us have particular ways of expressing our emotions based on our temperament, culture, and life experiences. However, given that the way you model expression of feelings will be your child's most powerful teacher, you must also determine if there are aspects of how you deal with anger that you would like to change. We emphasize again that you can and should talk to and coach your children about how to handle their anger appropriately; and you can and should carefully limit their exposure to violent television and video games. However, if you yourself routinely model unhealthy ways of expressing anger, you bury the positive guidance you are giving your children under the heavy mound of your own negative behavior. If you want children who can manage anger, the single most important thing you can do is teach them by good example.

This realization can be overwhelming for parents who wonder if their own skills measure up, day after day. None of us had perfect childhoods upon which to model our own behavior, and we're all at various stages of growth in our own lives. Children come along, and it is easy to feel discouraged: how can we help but pass on our own unresolved problems to our children? However, there is a more positive way to look at this dilemma. Children have a way of bringing out both the best and the worst in their parents. They shine a spotlight on those areas where we need to change. When we are willing to deal with those issues, we can grow in ways we may have never thought possible. We have the opportunity to resolve issues we might never have had the courage to address had we not had children.

So, how do you determine whether or not you express anger in a healthy manner that's a good model for your child? As honestly as you can, answer the questions in the exercise on page 92. While this exercise is not a scientific measurement, it can help you think about your own style of dealing with anger.

If these questions illuminated anger issues for you, you may be tempted to react in one of two extreme ways. On the one hand, you may feel hopeless and say to yourself, "I'll never be able to help my child if I have this many issues with anger." On the other hand, you may rationalize, "That's just me—I'm intense, I yell, it's just how I am. My kids know I love them." Both responses allow you to avoid addressing anger issues because they excuse you from taking action. And while your kids probably do know you love them, despite routine angry outbursts, they are learning from your behavior nonetheless.

Consult chapter eight for assistance in figuring out if expert professional help might be useful. You will find guidelines there for choosing a professional therapist.

Exercise: Evaluating Parental Anger

1. Do I raise my voice or yell when I'm frustrated more often than I would like?　☒ Yes　❑ No

2. Do I often say things when I'm angry that I regret later?　☒ Yes　❑ No

3. Do my kids lie to me to avoid my anger at something they've done?　❑ Yes　☒ No

4. Does my child behave in ways that concern me? Ways that he probably learned from me?　☒ Yes　❑ No

5. Am I sarcastic when I'm frustrated, instead of direct about my thoughts and feelings?　❑ Yes　☒ No

6. Do I use physical force against others in my family when I'm angry (pushing, jerking, hitting, etc.)　❑ Yes　☒ No

7. Have I ever caused property damage when I was angry?　❑ Yes　☒ No

8. Do other people think I have an "anger problem?"　❑ Yes　☒ No

9. Do I internalize my anger, causing it to surface as health problems?　❑ Yes　☒ No

10. Do I hold my anger in as long as I can, and then blow up?　❑ Yes　☒ No

11. When I'm angry, do I find sneaky (passive) ways to get back at people?　❑ Yes　☒ No

12. Do I use alcohol, drugs, or prescription medicines to mask my feelings?　❑ Yes　☒ No

13. Is the way I manage anger harming my relationships at work, or with friends or my partner?　☒ Yes　❑ No

Replacing Common Parental "Anger-isms"

You may feel like saying . . .	Instead, say . . .
"Am I the only one who ever picks anything up around here?"	"I'm feeling discouraged about this mess. I'd like you both to pick up your clothes and put them in the hamper."
"Get your filthy shoes off the couch! This is why we can't have nice things."	"I'm worried that you are going to get the couch dirty. Please keep your feet on the floor."
"What part of 'no' don't you understand?"	"I know you are disappointed that I said 'no.'" (Parent then removes self from the situation without further comment.)
"Knock it off!"	"The drumming on the back of my seat is irritating. Please stop."
"I have had it with you two!"	"I'm feeling frustrated right now. I'd like you to each go play in your own rooms, and we can work this out after we've all had some time to calm down."

Take a few moments to think of a few of your own "anger-isms." Create a replacement phrase for yourself and make a commitment to use it.

In addition to changing what you say, you may also need practice in following through with natural and logical consequences. (See chapter seven and Appendix D for help using these techniques.) Often the reason well-meaning parents finally blow up is because they have allowed their child's behavior to go on for too long. They have reached the breaking point in their patience. When you model a healthy verbalization of anger for your children *and* consistently set and follow through with clear boundaries, children learn to expect both empathy and limits.

Learning and implementing the skills you need to manage your own anger in healthy ways often feels overwhelming. Expect the process to take time, and expect that you will have good and bad days. Be as patient with yourself as you are with your child. Stay committed to your own growth: that is the most powerful catalyst for your child's growth.

PARENTAL SELF-CARE

While the skills you need to best manage your own anger are the same as the ones you have been learning about for your child, we recognize that the stresses you face are different. Adults must often be very creative to find time to do the things for ourselves and our relationships that keep us healthy and happy. Most of us agree that it's a good idea to relax and recharge, but we see it as a luxury when we get busy, and we push it aside. However, recent research has proven that those who take time to recharge actually get more done than those who don't. In other words, while it may seem counter-intuitive, people who regularly make time for self-care get more done in less time than those who doggedly keep pushing forward.

Parents often focus on the big week-long family vacation every year and neglect planning for smaller rejuvenating opportunities on a daily and weekly basis. Both are important for resting, relaxing, and recharging batteries so that life doesn't push you to anger. Just to get you started thinking about self-care, we've included some ideas.

Self-Care Ideas

Daily self-care
- Take time for coffee, tea, cocoa, or other warm refreshment
- Exercise vigorously for 20 minutes
- Read the newspaper or a book for 20 minutes
- Browse a favorite catalogue
- Write a letter or e-mail to a friend
- Explore the Internet for 20 minutes
- Use scented soap or lotion that you particularly enjoy
- Drink ice water with a slice of lemon

- Listen to music while you do chores
- Listen to a book on tape
- Meditate/pray for 20 minutes

Weekly self-care
- Take a bubble bath, surrounded by softly glowing candles
- Watch a favorite television program or video/dvd
- Prepare and eat a favorite meal
- Rent a movie and make popcorn
- Take a walk
- Call a friend or family member
- Work at a hobby or other creative pastime for an hour
- Go window shopping
- Attend a spiritual service
- Pick a favorite recording of a musical performance and do nothing but listen to it
- Play sports

Monthly self-care
- Go out to dinner without your kids
- See a movie with your partner
- Play a round of golf or go bowling
- Meet with a book club
- Have lunch with a friend
- Play cards or board games with friends
- Go hiking

Long-term self-care
- Plan and take a family vacation
- Get a babysitter and take a parent's weekend away
- Plan a "girls' night out" or a "guys' night out" with friends
- Go camping several times a year with or without the kids
- Take a class in an area of interest
- Participate in a community service project

Notice that the lists encompass varied aspects of caring for yourself: physical, social, emotional, intellectual, and spiritual. Paying attention to all these areas provides balance in your life as each area impacts and depends on the others. However, remember that it is especially important not to neglect your physical health. Eating healthy foods, getting enough sleep and exercise, and keeping up with basic medical care create the foundation on which all other aspects of self-care rest. Without the basics, you won't have the energy or the patience to care for children, especially angry ones.

Put a copy of the list on your refrigerator or bedroom mirror to remind yourself to *make time* to recharge. It is so easy to forget or neglect taking care of ourselves, but by making it a priority and putting reminders in highly visible locations, you can begin to make self-care a consistent part of your life.

PARENTING PARTNERS

If you are in a close relationship with a parenting partner, you may feel fortunate to have the support this relationship offers. You also know how much stress the arrival of children added to the relationship. Earlier we noted how children have a way of bringing to light our "unfinished business" as individuals. Often, even when two adults were able to discuss and agree upon parenting beliefs before having children, the reality of parenting brings out differences neither parent knew existed. Parents must consistently make communication a priority in order to work out their differences. Otherwise, they may find themselves in opposite corners of the ring where they attempt to overcorrect for the other's (perceived) strictness or lenience. This stance leads to a rift between partners, and causes family dysfunction in the long run.

If you feel that you and your partner struggle with co-parenting, being told "it's important to communicate" can feel frustrating. You may feel like answering, "That's great, but if we could do that, we wouldn't be having this problem in the first place!" The following "Five Laws of Co-Parenting" will help you create the foundation of a successful co-parenting relationship.

Five Laws of Co-Parenting

1. *We will make time to discuss and agree upon an overall parenting philosophy, and commit to learning and using methods of discipline that match our values.*

   If both parents complete the values checklist earlier in this chapter, their views can be a starting place for this discussion. Certain values may be more important for one than the other, and taking time to agree on how you will respect and support each other's priorities is essential to successful co-parenting. This exercise and conversation will also set the stage for you to agree upon which parenting skills you want to use on a daily basis.

2. *Unless safety is immediately at risk, we will not undermine each other's authority in front of our child.*

   Children are more successful when they see both parents as capable and empowered. When one or both routinely undermine the other, children may doubt the strength or credibility of their parent(s). As a result, they may be more defiant, manipulative, and divisive to get what they want. For the same reason, parents should take care not to undermine their own authority with statements such as, "Just wait until your father/ mother gets home!" This threat has the same effect on your authority as if your partner were saying it, creating the image in your child's mind of one parent as strong (and perhaps mean) and the other as weak.

3. *We will agree upon how we will ask for and offer help to each other during stressful moments with our child.*

   Just as it is important to refrain from undermining

your partner's interactions with your child, it is also essential to agree upon ways that you can each respectfully offer and ask for assistance at times when either of you is reaching the end of your patience. For example, one parent could say, "I'm feeling frustrated. Can you please help Jason get started with his homework?" Or "Is there anything I can do to help you right now?"

4. *We will discuss differences of opinion regarding parenting and discipline regularly, outside of our child's presence.*
  Your children can and should hear you respectfully negotiate simple differences of opinion, such as whether to fly or drive to a vacation destination, with your partner. However, discussions about parenting differences should be held out of the earshot of children.

5. *We will respect and show appreciation for each other's agreed upon role within the family.*
  Simply put, this last "law" is what holds everything together. Find a balance that both parents feel good about in dividing the many tasks required to run your household. Regularly recognize and acknowledge the unique contributions of each parent.

Discussing and customizing these agreements for your relationship is the first step. This conversation is a great opportunity for you and your partner to practice using I-messages, communicating primary emotions to each other regarding what is important to you as a parent. In Appendix F, you will find a blank form to use in creating your own unique agreement. Do the exercise as part of self-care: get a babysitter and go out for dinner or away for a weekend. Use the time to reconnect while you develop your own co-parenting agreement. We suggest posting the result next to your self-care list. You will be amazed at the power of these two documents to improve your co-parenting relationship and ultimately reduce the stress and anger that can come with parenthood.

SOCIAL SUPPORT

Parenthood, by its very nature, is about relationships. In addition to your parenting partner, there can be many other relationships in your life that support you throughout the years of being a parent. Close friends, extended family, childcare providers, teachers, coaches, and even social acquaintances can help create the web of relationships that parents need to avoid making the parenting journey alone.

Healthy social relationships rejuvenate us, validate our experiences, and keep us from feeling isolated. Beyond that, there is enormous value in having a space where you can safely complain and have a good cry or a rollicking laugh.

During the parenting years it is particularly important to be purposeful in choosing which friendships or extended family members deserve your energy and time. This is not about being selfish or uncaring towards those relationships in your life that tend to drain you; it is frankly about self-preservation. Children need us in so many legitimate ways that consume our physical and emotional energy. Being emotionally present and calm with our children requires that we do our best to guard our energy in the places where we have some control.

The more adult relationships you have in your life where you feel criticized or compelled to give of your time or emotional support without much in the way of reciprocity only makes it more difficult to be successful as a parent. "You can't nurture from an empty cup" applies here. This doesn't necessarily mean you have to cut all ties with friends or extended family who are either needy or critical, but it does mean that you are aware of those relationships and find ways to set limits within them.

At the same time, this is a life stage where mutually supportive friendships are especially important. It takes time to develop a relationship with a great degree of comfort and trust. However, once you have a sense of which of your relationships you want to nurture, you can begin to put that time into those.

Characteristics of a Rejuvenating Friendship

- Shared values, parenting beliefs, and goals
- Freedom to share one's mistakes openly, without fear of criticism
- Trust in each other's judgment and positive intentions
- Shared interests to some extent
- Shared sense of humor about life
- No pressure to glamorize one's life
- Trust that confidences will be respected
- Equal give-and-take over time
- Safe place to complain, brag, and ask for help
- Sense of support and mutual enjoyment

In chapter seven, we have stressed the importance of healthy anger management strategies for parents. We've also discussed ways parents can care for themselves in order to reduce their own anger while dealing with children. In chapter eight, we will discuss how to determine if your family or child needs expert professional help.

POINTS TO REMEMBER

- The most important way to help a child manage anger is to learn to manage your own anger in healthy ways.
- Define and prioritize your family values; be sure your behavior reflects them.
- Self-care is a necessity, not a luxury, on a daily, weekly, monthly, and long-term basis. Make time for it.
- Discuss and apply the "Five Laws of Co-Parenting"with your partner.

8

Help! Nothing Is Working

So far you've learned about normal, healthy anger, and ex-
plored why some children might seem angrier than others.
You've learned skills to help your child express anger appropriately and to solve problems. You've even looked at
ways you can reduce and manage your own intense feelings, so that you can stay calm when helping him with his
anger and be a good role model on a day-to-day basis.

There are three important areas to consider when you
feel that despite your efforts, your child continues to struggle. First, how long and how consistently have you used
the skills you've learned in this book? Second, does your
family need outside help? Finally, might your child need
professional evaluation and treatment? This chapter will
help you determine what the next steps are for your child
and family.

DON'T GIVE UP TOO SOON

Having an angry child can make you feel a bit like something is on fire. A perfectly normal parental response is to want to put out the "fire" immediately. However, the one thing parents consistently underestimate is how long it takes for change to occur, both in their own parenting as well as in their child's angry, out-of-control behavior.

A more helpful analogy to replace putting out a fire is that of planting a tree seedling. Once you've planted the seedling, it requires sunlight, water, nutrients, weeding, pruning, and most important, *time to grow*. To change behavior, parents and children also need time to grow. It is not unreasonable for you to have to do the same thing—respond in a new way yourself or ask your child to apply a new skill—*fifty to seventy-five times* before the behavior becomes second nature for either one of you. When you have a realistic view of how long it takes for change to occur, you can be more patient with yourself and your child.

Time to grow

The first part of reevaluating what you've tried is making sure your time frame for change is realistic. Our experience is that parents often feel understandably impatient about wanting to see change. Consequently, they often give up on the skills before they or the child has used them long enough to become competent. When you find yourself ready to give up and slip back into old patterns of responding to your anger or your child's, review some of the examples in this book, find other parenting information that encourages you, or refer again to chapter seven about taking care of yourself so that you can bring your best effort to your child.

Consistency

The second half of re-evaluating what you've tried starts with being as objective as possible about how consistently you've used the skills. In the hustle and bustle of daily life, it can be easy to slip back into old behaviors, especially in times of stress. During the years we were part of a treatment team working with behaviorally disturbed preschoolers, we built in a "self-check" process to our treatment planning in order to hold ourselves accountable for consistently using the skills. We would always evaluate our own consistency before we considered a change in a child's treatment plan, knowing that especially with very challenging children, it is easy for adults to fall back into old ways of doing things.

An easy way to determine how consistently you are using your new positive skills is to use a simple tally sheet. Choose one skill to focus on at a time, such as using I-messages, active listening, or empathizing with your child's feelings. Make two columns on an 8½ by 11-inch paper. Label one column "Yes" and the other "No." Ask your parenting partner to closely observe your behavior over one to two days (or you can do this yourself), and mark a tally for each time you use that particular skill, and another for each time you slip into old patterns. Once you get to the point where eighty percent of your responses are "Yes," congratulate yourself! *However, you should still expect several months to pass before lasting change will begin to take place in your child. This may feel discouraging, but again remember that you are not putting out a fire, you are growing a tree.*

WHEN FAMILIES NEED OUTSIDE HELP

Many times we are able to deal effectively with family difficulties on our own. At other times, trusted friends or clergy can offer the support and guidance we need. However, there are times and circumstances when we need the support, neutral perspective, and expertise of a professional. For a variety of reasons, people often hesitate to seek out mental health support for far too long. They may feel that seeing a therapist is an admission of weakness or failure on their part. Or they may fear feeling a sense of judgment from an outsider. And frankly, many people feel embarrassed about sharing their personal problems with a stranger. Yet there are situations when your family's health needs to override these fears and hesitancies.

In chapter one, we discussed possible medical and developmental causes for anger in children. While these causes do not have family factors at the root, they can still create an enormous amount of stress within a family. It is not uncommon for families coping with a child who has a special need, such as autism, to find themselves responding to their child more negatively over time. Lack of support, worry, exhaustion, and discouragement are just a few of the factors that can take a toll on a marriage and a family. In these situations, a family therapist can offer parents support, and also provide concrete skills that will help parents and children cope. Remember that asking for help is not a sign of failure. In fact, it is an excellent way to model healthy problem solving for your child.

In other cases, family events create the potential for stress and chaos, resulting in increased anger in children. For example, divorce is inherently upsetting to children. However, when parents argue and speak poorly about each other in their children's presence, the negative effects become continuous, giving the child no chance to grieve and recover from the trauma. Sometimes adults pass in and out of children's lives in ways that are out of their control, such as when a single parent has new significant relationships that are not stable. Other examples of circumstances that create chaos for children may include unpredictable schedules and routines, inconsistency in discipline from one or between parents, or a parent who has chronic mental health needs. Again, an objective and helpful family therapist can offer guidance on parenting and managing divorce and blended family issues, along with support in managing your own emotions.

Of most concern is when serious, ongoing family problems are the cause of a child's extreme anger. If a member of your family is abusing drugs or alcohol, or if there is violence of any kind within your home, these problems must be addressed before you can expect your child to make significant changes. You may be tempted to focus on your child's behavior rather than adult behavior in the home; however, this is as ineffective as putting a small bandage over a gaping wound. There is no way around it—the underlying problem must be addressed with a professional.

Sometimes it's hard to decide when a child's behavior warrants specific attention by a professional. Whether the child's behavior results from something within the child, is due to past trauma, or is related to ongoing family issues, the information below will help guide you in determining when to seek outside help for your child. Any one of the behaviors listed suggests your child may have serious emotional problems that should be assessed by a professional as quickly as possible.

Signs a child needs immediate professional help
- intense and frequent anger in many different environments (home, day care, school, sports, play dates, etc.)
- risky behavior
- aggressive or violent behavior
- excessive lying or stealing
- severe withdrawal or depression
- self-injury or threats of suicide
- alcohol or drug use
- anorexia or bulimia
- excessive anxiety, hoarding food or possessions, or compulsive behavior
- fire setting
- acting out sexually
- cruelty to animals
- smearing feces

Even when your child does not display these particular behaviors, you may be concerned. Trust your parental instincts and consult a professional. Choosing a professional who is qualified and with whom you and your family feel comfortable can be a confusing, even daunting, process.

We have included here some guidelines that you can use to evaluate accessibility and qualifications.

Guidelines for Choosing a Professional Therapist

Practical considerations

- Does my insurance cover mental health counseling? If so, how many sessions are covered?
- Is the therapist I'm considering a preferred provider in my plan?
- What is the therapist's hourly rate? Is there a sliding fee scale?
- Is his/her location convenient for me?
- What is appointment availability? Does it fit our schedule?
- If I feel my child may need it, does the therapist offer after-hours or crisis care?

Questions to ask when interviewing a potential therapist

- What are your degrees? Are you licensed?
  (These professionals are qualified to work with children and families: psychiatrists, M.D.; psychologists, Ph.D.; counselors, M.S. or M.A.; clinical social workers, M.S.W.; and marriage and family therapists, M.F.T. You can and should check a therapist's credentials. Every health provider must be licensed in his/her field in the state he/she practices in. Ask for his/her license number and then call the State Department of Health or search for the provider's status on your state's Web site.)
- Are you trained or experienced in working with children? How many years have you been working with children?
- What methods do you use in therapy? Have they been proven effective for problems such as my child's?
- What is your philosophy about medication for children?
- How will I be involved in my child's therapy?

Determining if the therapist is a good fit for your family

- Does he/she put you on edge, or make you feel comfortable?

- Does he/she ask questions to learn more about you and your situation?
- Does he/she listen to what you're saying, carefully considering your perceptions of the problem and your goals for your child/family?
- Does he/she ask you enough questions to fully understand your child's early development, as well as the current concern?

Remember that feeling comfortable with your therapist is critical to successful therapy. Take time to think about how you feel about the therapist after your meeting has ended. Be sure this is a person with whom you can easily talk, and whom you like and respect.

In this chapter we've discussed the steps you can take when you feel that the efforts you are making to help your child are not working, including reevaluating what you've tried and for how long, and determining if your family or your child needs outside help.

Parenting children who have difficulty with anger or other intense emotions can be exhausting and often discouraging. Please remember to take care of yourself in ways that are meaningful to you. *Remember that taking care of yourself is taking care of your family.*

Learning to manage anger in healthy ways is a life-long process. Your goal for yourself and your child is progress, not perfection. Congratulate yourself for coming this far. As you proceed, we wish you patience, perseverance, humor, and an occasional night out for dinner and a movie! Best of success to you and your child.

POINTS TO REMEMBER

- Get outside support when you need it—it can make a difference for you and your child.
- Helping an angry child is more like growing a tree than putting out a fire. Be patient as your child grows.

Though it may feel like putting out
a fire, parenting an angry child is much
more like growing a tree.

Appendices

A. The Face of Anger at Each Developmental Stage   110

B. Factors that May Affect Attachment   120

C. Practical Questions About Time-Out   121

D. Getting Started with Conflict Management   124

E. Steps to Implement a Reinforcement System   128

F. Co-Parenting Agreement   130

G. How Skillfully Do You Manage Anger Worksheet   132

Recommended Reading   134

Index   137

APPENDIX A

The Face of Anger at Each Developmental Stage

(Pages 110 to 119)

INFANCY

The primary task in infancy is developing a sense of trust, security, and safety. Parents provide this by offering predictable nurturing, as well as through hundreds of small, positive reciprocal interactions throughout the course of each day. This is a crucial time where the foundation of the parent-child relationship is laid. The quality of this relationship impacts every aspect of a child's development.

Parents can begin labeling emotions for the infant long before it appears that he can understand the meaning of the words. When the parent responds to an infant's cries with an empathetic facial expression and tone of voice, and verbalizes for him the primary emotion, the parent begins teaching the infant how to access, identify, and express his feelings. He also learns that his feelings are accepted and that he can view his parent as a source of comfort and guidance.

In the following chart, examples of infants' emotional expression and healthy parental responses are described. It is important to remember that since crying is the infant's only method of communication, it is a parent's role to respond and learn to interpret the child's needs.

Infants – Setting the Stage for Emotional Development

Event	Infant Response	Parental Response	Infant Learns
Carly, 3 mo., wakes up hungry during the night.	She cries loudly. Her face becomes red and her body is rigid.	Mother picks her up, pats her back, and in an empathetic voice says, "Oh, honey, I bet you're hungry."	I can communicate to get my needs met. My feelings are important. My mother is dependable. The world is a safe place.
Parker, 7 mo., picks up a glass Christmas ornament. His father takes it away.	Parker cries.	Father empathizes, "You look sad. You wanted to play with that shiny ball. Here's your favorite rattle!"	My father cares how I feel, and he will keep me safe.
Cole, 11 mo., grabs the cat's tail, and the cat scratches him.	He screams in shock and pain.	Mother picks him up, examines and kisses the scratch. She says, "Oh, ouch, that hurt you."	I can ask for comfort when I get hurt, and my mother will care for me.

TODDLER YEARS

During the toddler years, children are beginning to figure out the world and their place in it. They are able to begin to understand cause and effect, are building their ability to communicate, and are becoming increasingly motivated to be independent.

Anyone who has parented a toddler would agree that typical toddlers are passionate, obstinate, and not terribly reasonable. Part of helping them toward the goal of healthy emotional expression is to provide them with the skills they need to recognize and communicate their feelings. Just as it is important for a child to be able to label a cat, horse, or pig, they also need to be able to recognize and express sad, angry, hurt, scared, and their many other feelings.

Parents can also begin to teach some beginning skills in self-calming. Your toddler can learn to take deep breaths, count to three, sing a song, and many other skills that will point him in the direction of developing self-management skills.

The following table includes examples of how a parent might help a toddler develop skills for healthy emotional expression, and begin to lay the groundwork for problem solving.

Toddlers – Building Skills for Emotional Expression

Event	Toddler's Response	Parental Response	What the Toddler Learns
Tatum, 14 mo., excitedly vocalizes and motions toward something, but Mother cannot understand what she wants.	She begins yelling the same "words," starts to scream, and throws herself on the kitchen floor.	Mom picks her up and says, "I don't know what you want, honey. It looks like you are frustrated." Mother strokes Tatum's head, and then distracts her with a toy.	Even though my mom can't always give me what I want, she still cares about my feelings, and helps me handle them.
Keegan, 17 mo., wants a glass of juice, and is having a hard time waiting for his dad to pour it.	He stomps his feet and screams, "Juice, juice, juice!"	Dad says, "I know, it's hard to wait. Juice is coming. Let's sing the waiting song!"	Dad cares about my wants and needs. He understands my feelings, is helping to me learn what I am feeling and to handle my frustration.
Carter, 2½ yr., is attempting to build a block tower, which keeps falling over.	He screams and throws a block across the room.	Mom scoops him up into her lap and says, "Wow, you look mad. It's okay to be mad, and it's not okay to throw the blocks. Let's take two deep breaths to calm down, and maybe together we can build that tower."	Mom cares about how I feel, and she will set limits when I lose control. She will help me learn to calm down and find ways to solve the problem."

PRESCHOOL/KINDERGARTEN

During the preschool and kindergarten years, you will find that your child is more anxious to please and has greater self-control. She has a greater ability to verbally express herself, and, if given the right tools, is capable of using both self-calming and beginning problem-solving skills. Also during this time, children develop a greater capacity for empathy for others and better social skills.

A parent can begin teaching a child to express emotions and to problem solve. Though it continues to be important to help your child identify and label her feelings, if she has been given the tools and vocabulary for emotional expression during her first three years, it is likely that she will often be able to do this independently, or with just a cue or reminder from you.

The following examples show the ways that parents can now combine the skills of emotional expression with problem solving.

Preschool / Kindergarten – Building Skills for Problem Solving

Event	Child's Response	Parental Response	Child Learns
Jessie, 3½ yr., is saying goodbye to her favorite playmate with whom she spent the afternoon.	She cries, pulls away from her mother, saying, "I don't want to go home!"	Mom crouches down, looks in Jessie's eyes and says, "Are you sad about leaving your friend? It's hard to say goodbye. Can you walk by yourself to the car, or would you like to hold my hand?"	It's okay for me to be sad and to show my feelings. My mom cares how I feel; she will still provide structure and limits.
Trevor, 5 yr., has recently learned to tie his shoes, but is finding it difficult today.	He is beginning to get tense and says, "Stupid shoelace!"	Dad sits on the floor next to Trevor and says, "It looks like you are getting discouraged. Learning to tie shoes can be hard. Now would be a great time to take three deep breaths and count to 5."	I can calm down my feelings to finish difficult tasks. My dad is there to teach and coach me; he also believes I can do it myself.
Grace, 6 yr., is frightened when, during a storm, the electricity goes out.	She cries from her room, and yells, "Mommy, I'm scared!"	Mom comes to her room and reassures, "I'm glad you let me know you're scared. It's okay, the storm just made the lights go out for a while. What do you think you need to feel safe?"	I can tell my mom how I am feeling, and she will give me the information I need help me feel safe. She will give me the support I need to come up with solutions.

EARLY ELEMENTARY

By this time, a child has had some life experience which has given her more opportunities to practice managing disappointment, tolerating frustration, and controlling her impulses better than in her preschool years. In addition, a more advanced vocabulary and the ability to understand and practice basic problem solving gives her a greater ability to manage anger constructively.

Based on the new skills a child at this age is developing, a parent's role in helping her manage feelings will begin to change. Parents' challenge during this time is to balance this shift from "teacher" to "coach" in a way that is consistent with their child's personality, skills, and maturity within a given situation. In the previous stage, parents were accustomed to being ready to offer suggestions and solutions to build to the child's skills. During this stage it is often better for the parent to be a good listener, letting the child think things through out loud, allowing her to come up with her own ideas and solutions, remembering that a child may still need some guidance about how to handle new situations.

The role of parents in the early elementary years is to help their child build the skills to assertively communicate thoughts and feelings to others, to become successful in social problem solving, and continue to help their child fine-tune the skills she needs to manage the intense emotions.

Early Elementary – Applying and Practicing Skills

Event	Child's Response	Parental Response	Child Learns
Eli, 7 yr., and his sister are playing video games. He is waiting for his turn.	He gets mad that it's taking too long, stomps to his room, saying, "It's not fair, I hate you!" and slams the door.	Mom waits a few minutes, then joins him in his room. She says, "I wonder if you were worried that you weren't going to get a turn? I like how you took yourself to your room to calm down. What else could you do to solve the problem?"	Mom cares about how I feel; she does not rescue me from my feelings and problems. She coaches me to find my own solutions.
Kate, 8 yr., is teased at school about her new glasses.	She storms into the house after school and declares, "I hate these glasses, and I'm never wearing them again!"	Dad puts an arm around her shoulder and says, "I can see you are pretty sad. Do you want to talk about it?"	Dad supports me when I'm feeling sad, gives me the opportunity to talk through my feelings, and lets me decide how much help I need.
Silas, 9 yr., strikes out for the third time during his baseball game.	He tells his parents, "I hate baseball, I'm not playing anymore."	Dad empathizes with Silas about the game and his feelings, and says, "Let's talk more about this when you are feeling better." Later, Dad helps Silas consider alternative solutions to quitting.	I can be angry and feel discouraged. My dad will support me in my feelings, and help me solve problems, while challenging me not to give up.

MIDDLE CHILDHOOD

During middle childhood, children are becoming more logical and responsible. They are much more able to independently use the skills learned at earlier stages. They are beginning the transition from childhood to adolescence. They have original ideas and are able to make plans, develop their own opinions, assert leadership and independence, and understand abstract thinking. During this time, they also become concerned with living their life by a moral code, and focus more on judgments and decisions being fair and justified. As they near adolescence, they may begin to resent parental control. Earlier self-confidence may fluctuate with periods of moodiness and self-doubt.

Many children will have reached some level of mastery in skills to manage and communicate their emotions and to solve problems in middle childhood. They will need fewer cues and directives from parents to handle difficult situations. This is the time when a parent's role begins to shift from "coach" to what will eventually become that of "supporter" in adolescence. However, it is also a time when sudden regressions in emotions, judgment, and behavior are not uncommon as children near preadolescence, and parents may find themselves needing to frequently adjust their responses to match the need.

Middle Childhood – Developing Confidence in Skills

Event	Child's Response	Parental Response	Child Learns
Caleb, 10 yr., comes home after having had an argument with his friend, Jason.	He stomps into the house, saying "I don't even know why I hang out with Jason. He is so bossy."	Mom says, "Sounds like you are feeling kind of discouraged about your friend. Let me know if you need to talk."	My mom cares and is there to support me if I need her.
Lindsay, 11 yr., found out that one of her friends wrote a mean note about her to another friend.	She bursts into tears as she runs up the stairs, saying, "I hate my life! I'm going to have to get all new friends."	Dad says, "You must have had a rough day. I'm here if you need me."	Dad cares about how I feel. He gives me room to deal with things on my own, and offers support if I need it.
Madison, 12 yr., wants her mother to buy her expensive shoes, and Mom says, "no."	Madison stomps out of the store, saying, "I never get anything cool. All my friends have them. You don't even care how I feel."	Mom waits until they get home, and says, "You seemed sad and disappointed earlier at the mall. Would you like to talk about it?"	I may not always get my way, and my mom cares about how I feel.

Factors that May Affect Attachment

Parent's
- Lack of understanding of child development
- Emotional immaturity in parent
- Inconsistent responses to child's needs and cues
- Unresolved childhood issues in parent
- Personality or temperamental mismatches between parent and child
- Postpartum depression
- Extended illness in the parent or child
- Developmental or mental health issues in the parent or child
- Parental stress
- Lack of support from friends or family
- Extended work hours
- Marital stress
- Poverty
- Divorce
- Domestic violence

Child's
- Extended separation of child from parent
- Inadequate (non-responsive) child care
- Physical, sexual, or verbal abuse
- Neglect
- Parental drug or alcohol use
- Foster care
- Adoption issues
- Death of a parent

APPENDIX C

Practical Questions About Time-Out

Q. *I've been using my son's room for time-outs, but he plays with his toys when he's in there. My mother-in-law says I should put him in the bathroom instead. What do you think?*

Some people suggest using another room in the house, such as the bathroom, so that the child doesn't associate his bedroom with punishment. However, remember that the goal of time-out is for a child to calm down so that he can successfully engage in problem solving. Playing with his toys may be soothing to your child, so we suggest not worrying about it. Just be sure to follow through with helping your son talk about his feelings when he is calm and/or solving the problem that caused him to lose control in the first place.

Where your child goes for time-out depends on what room is safest and most calming. For some children, the fewer distractions in a room, the better. If your child is routinely angry, consider making some temporary changes, such as emptying a guest room as much as possible, to provide a calm space.

Q. *When I take my out-of-control daughter to time-out, she rushes the door when I try to leave the room. I'm afraid I'm going to pinch her fingers accidently, and I feel terrible that I have to nearly shove her out of the way to get the door closed. What should I do?*

Any parent who has attempted to help an angry, out-of-control child to time-out will agree that it is a daunting task. Here's what to do: use your body as a block between your child and the doorway. Back through the doorway, leaning forward toward your child, using one hand to gently and firmly grasp both her wrists as you inch the door closed. Carefully pull your arm out and be careful not to let your own fingers get caught in the door. Always tell your child she is not in trouble, she just needs to calm down, and over time these struggles will disappear. If you still cannot get your child to time-out safely for both of you, feel that being alone is too frightening for your child, or fear that the child may hurt herself or the room, consider *holding* her instead. (See pages 55–56.)

Q. *When my daughter is in her room for a time-out, she is so angry that she throws her toys against the door and even sometimes breaks things. How do I handle this?*

You have two choices: put her in a bare room where there is nothing she can throw or let her experience the natural consequences of breaking her toys. In the second choice, your role is to empathize with her about the broken toy so that she can make the connection between the loss of the toy and her own behavior. Do not lecture her or buy her a replacement toy. If she damages the house or property that isn't hers, require her to help fix it or replace it in whatever way that is developmentally appropriate.

Q. *My son refuses to stay in his room for a time-out. I've been told to add on minutes when he leaves his room, but it becomes a never-ending power struggle. Is there another way to deal with this?*

Many people are uncomfortable with the idea of standing on the other side of the door to hold it shut for the length of time it takes for a child to calm down (the length of the time-out). However, we think that by holding the door shut, you create an uninterrupted period for your child to calm down without continually re-engaging you negatively. This practice is more in keeping with the spirit of time-out, while adding minutes is punitive and does nothing to stop the negative interaction.

Q. *My child is too big for me to assist to time-out. What can I do?*

Safety is important for both you and your child. Do not struggle with a child who is too big for you to assist to time-out. (If you are the parent of a young child, you can see why it is important to begin teaching anger management skills early in life!) Unfortunately, as the parent of an older child, your options are limited while the child is out of control. You may need to seek outside help. Go to chapter eight, "Help! Nothing Is Working."

Getting Started with Conflict Management

Q. *Are there any rules or guidelines I should set up before introducing conflict management?*

The main rules for conflict management are probably already a part of the basic family values you are teaching.

- Agree to solve the problem
- Be honest
- Take turns talking
- Use kind words

It helps to post a word and picture chart with these four rules on the refrigerator or other common area. They will look "official" and can be referred to easily during problem solving.

Q. *Is there any way I can help motivate my child to try conflict management? He/she doesn't seem interested.*

Like all of us, children may resist change. Setting up a reinforcement system with a specific goal is a great way to encourage kids to "try on" a new behavior. Once the child has built some confidence and skills in this new way of handling conflict, he/she will begin to be reinforced socially. When this happens, external reinforcements can be phased out. Refer to "Steps to Implement a Reinforcement System" in Appendix E for detailed instructions.

Q. *What if my child keeps interrupting, or refuses to listen to me or other family members?*

This is most common when first starting the process,

because most children fear that adult intervention will result in someone getting in trouble, and they are protecting themselves. This behavior will most likely stop once kids begin to trust the process. In the meantime, remind and reassure the child that he will get a turn to talk, and be sure that he does. It can also be helpful to say to him, "You're not in trouble, we just need to solve the problem." However, if a child continues to interrupt or refuses to listen to the other child, it is important to empathetically enforce the stated rules. You might say, "It looks like you're having a tough time problem solving right now. We'll try again later." Then, depending on the problem at hand, make a decision that reinforces the other child's willingness to problem solve without shaming the child who wasn't able to follow the process.

Q. *What if my daughter gets verbally or physically aggressive while we're trying to solve the problem?*

If you think she needs more than a gentle reminder of the conflict management rules, then it is important to recognize that she is not calm enough to problem solve. Tell her: "It looks like you're not feeling calm enough to solve the problem right now; we'll try again in a few minutes." Refer to chapter four for skills you can use to help children manage their intense emotions. If you have a second child who is patiently waiting and ready to problem solve, be sure to thank her for doing so. After a few minutes, approach the child who was out of control, praising her for calming down, and ask if she is ready to solve the problem. It can be tempting to "let sleeping dogs lie" once everyone has calmed down. The kids perhaps have moved on to something else, and you've achieved some much deserved peace. However, in the spirit of ensuring that children build trust in this new process, it is essential to return to the issue.

Q. *I have an 18-month-old and a 5-year-old. I'd like to start conflict management, but how can I do it with one child this young?*

It is a great idea to start this when children are very young, though it takes a bit more creativity and theatrical flair on your part. We have found that the most effective method is to speak for the 18-month-old while problem solving with the older child. You can act as both facilitator and narrator—asking the questions of each child, and using a childlike voice to respond appropriately on the behalf of the toddler. By doing this, you give your 5-year-old the opportunity to practice the skills, and your younger child hears the language you want him to eventually use. This is also a wonderful way to begin building a positive relationship between the two children.

Q. *How do I handle lying?*

The reassuring thing about this kind of conflict management is that it is not your role to be judge and jury regarding who is telling the truth. The focus is on helping kids air their feelings and find mutually agreeable solutions to the problem. You can begin by saying, "It looks like you two have very different ideas about what happened. I wasn't here. I don't know what happened. But I can tell you both have big feelings about it, and I'm sure we can solve the problem." Then start with step 2 of the conflict management guidelines and work toward a resolution. We certainly do not intend to suggest that lying is okay; rather your focus in the moment of conflict is to help kids work toward solutions. As with any family value, teaching about honesty will happen at more neutral times in family life.

Q. *What should I do if I'm in a situation where I can't stop right that moment to help facilitate problem solving between my children?*

We would like to say, "Stop and do it anyway." But

the reality is that there are times when schedules, the environment, or your energy level and patience suggest that now may not be the best time for problem solving. These times should truly be a rarity, knowing that kids will most effectively integrate the values and skills associated with problem solving when you place a high priority on them, and consistently work with the children to gain mastery over the process. However, if on rare occasions you need to intervene in a conflict by saying, "I can see you two are having a problem deciding who will get to sit in the front seat, and it's important in our family that we find ways to work problems out. But right now we need to get into the car so we can get to our doctor's appointment on time. This time I'm going to make a decision that Jacob ride in the front seat on the way there, and Sabrina ride there on the way home. When we get home, we will see what ideas you both can come up with for how to handle this problem next time."

Q. *What if a child has broken an important family rule or value?*

   This is where the art, rather than the science of parenting comes in. A good question to ask yourself is: Is this a time for helping my child learn and practice social problem solving? Or have our basic family rules been broken to the point that I feel my child needs a clear limit and consequence about an important family value, such as no tolerance for verbal or physical violence? Sometimes, you may choose to ignore a small inappropriate behavior in order to focus on helping kids work out a problem. Later you can talk with a child who has hit his sister, perhaps by starting to work with him more on some of the social skills. You may even require some sort of consequence or restitution on his part that is logically related to what he did to his sister. Other times, you may decide that a consequence is needed more immediately, and return to problem solving afterwards.

Steps to Implement a Reinforcement System

1. Decide on a specific behavioral goal for your child. Put it in words your child can understand. State the goal in the positive ("do this") instead of the negative ("don't do this").
   Examples
   "Use words to say how you feel."
   "Use kind hands and words."
   "Take a deep breath and calm down."

2. Choose either a sticker chart (for younger children) or marble jar (for older children) as the way to measure the child's progress toward earning the reinforcement. Also, with the child's input, make a list of items or activities the child may earn.

3. Sit down with your child to explain the goal.
   Example
   "Jeremy, I've noticed that sometimes it's hard for you to remember to use kind hands with your sister when you are frustrated. I know this can be hard to learn, and I want to help make it easier for you. On this poster, it says, 'Use kind hands and words,' and there is a picture of a boy playing nicely with his sister. Today, we can go to the store and you can pick out whatever stickers you like the best. Each time I notice you using kind hands and words with your sister, we will put a sticker on this chart next to the poster. When you have earned (10, 20, 30 stickers, depending on the age of the child), you can choose a special item or activity from this list."
   Note: For some kids, just the act of putting the sticker on (or marble in the jar) is enough reinforcement. Other

times, children may need a reward. For parents who prefer not to give tangible rewards, such as a small toy or treat, time spent with you doing something fun (playing a game or trips to the park, playground, museum, zoo, etc.) can be excellent rewards, too.

4. Reinforce, reinforce, reinforce! Initially, reward the child every time you see the desired behavior. Later drop to an intermittent reward schedule (slowly decrease how frequently you reward, but in a nonpredictable pattern).

Be sure to offer verbal praise, physical touch (hugs, etc.), and lots of excitement and animation so that your child experiences the social reinforcement along with the tangible rewards.

When your child has accomplished the goal you set, go on to the next thing you want him or her to work on.

5. Have one or two goals at a time. More than that is confusing to your child and hard for you to keep track of.

Co-Parenting Agreement

1. We will make time to discuss and agree upon an overall parenting philosophy, and commit to learning and using methods of discipline that match our values.

   Our most important values are:

   - _Independence_   • _Caring_
   - _honesty_   • _respectful_
   - _flexibility_   • _hardworking_

   The primary methods of discipline we agree to use are:

   - _time out_
   - _removing computer / phone_
   - _removing family fun_
   - _____
   - _____

2. Unless safety is an immediate risk, we will not undermine each other's authority in front of our child.

3. We will agree upon how we will ask for and offer help to each other during stressful moments with our child.

   To ask for or offer help, we will:

   - _____
   - _____

- _____

- _____

4. We will discuss differences of opinion regarding parenting and discipline regularly, outside of our child's presence.

5. We will respect and show appreciation for each other's agreed-upon role within the family.
   The ways we each like to be shown appreciation are:

- _Family meeting_____

- _aknowledging something positive_

- _every day_____

- _____

- _____

- _____

- _____

- _____

APPENDIX G

How Skillfully
Do You Manage Anger?

Think about a time recently when you felt angry, and answer the
following questions.

1. What was the situation?

   _When I asked Lily to stop
   following me and touching me and
   pulling on me_

2. What was your primary feeling or thought? ① _fear that I_

   ② _fear that she well not stop_ _am_
   and I ③ will have to deal _feeling_
   with yelling, physical harm.
   Fear that she is spoilled

3. What was your secondary feeling or thought?

   anger, resentment, feeling
   used, feeling sorry for
   myself.

4. What did you say or do?

   I screamed, pushed her
   away, locked myself
   in the bathroom and stopped
   talking to her.

5. Identify as many skills as you can that helped you deal with the situation and describe what you did:

❑ life experience   ❑ frustration tolerance

❑ impulse control   ❑ problem-solving skills

I just removed myself
and I was not very effective.
I wished I could mirror her
or hold her when she
asked me to hold her

6. Did you use all the skills? Did you use them to your satisfaction?

_No_

7. What will you do now to manage anger more effectively?

① try to hold her
② try to name her feelings
③ try to put myself in
her shoes.

Recommended Reading

General Parenting

- *Active Parenting: Teaching Cooperation, Courage, and Responsibility* by Michael Popkin, Ph.D. San Francisco: HarperSanFrancisco, 1987.
- *Ages and Stages: A Parent's Guide to Normal Childhood Development* by Charles E. Schaefer, Ph.D., and Theresa Foy DiGeronimo. New York: John Wiley & Sons, 2000.
- *Dealing with Disappointment: Helping Kids Cope When Things Don't Go Their Way* by Elizabeth Crary. Seattle: Parenting Press, 2003.
- *The Explosive Child: A New Approach for Understanding and Parenting Easily Frustrated, Chronically Inflexible Children* by Ross W. Greene, Ph.D. New York: Quill/HarperCollins, 2005.
- *Growing Up Again: Parenting Ourselves, Parenting Our Children*, 2nd ed., by Jean Illsley Clarke and Connie Dawson. Center City, Minn.: Hazelden Publishing, 1998.
- *Is This a Phase? Child Development & Parent Strategies, Birth to 6 Years* by Helen F. Neville. Seattle: Parenting Press, 2007.
- *Mentor Manager, Mentor Parent: How to Develop Responsible People and Build Successful Relationships at Work and at Home* by Linda Culp Dowling and Cecile Culp Mielenz, Ph.D. Burneyville, Okla.: Comcon Books, 2002.
- *Parenting from the Inside Out: How a Deeper Self-Understanding Can Help You Raise Children Who Thrive* by Daniel J. Siegal, M.D., and Mary Hartzell, M.Ed. New York: Jeremy P. Tarcher/Penguin, 2004.
- *Pick Up Your Socks . . . and Other Skills Growing Children Need!* by Elizabeth Crary. Seattle: Parenting Press, 1990.
- *Positive Discipline*, rev. ed., by Jane Nelson, Ed.D. New York: Valentine Books, 1996.
- *Raising Your Spirited Child: A Guide for Parents Whose*

Child Is More Intense, Sensitive, Perceptive, Persistent, and Energetic, rev. ed., by Mary Sheedy Kurcinka. New York: Harper Perennial, 1998.
- *Time-In: When Time-Out Doesn't Work* by Jean Illsley Clarke, Ph.D. Seattle: Parenting Press, 1999.
- *Without Spanking or Spoiling: A Practical Approach to Toddler and Preschool Guidance*, rev. ed., by Elizabeth Crary. Seattle: Parenting Press, 1993.

Adult Anger Management and Self-Care
- *The Anger Control Workbook* by Matthew McKay, Ph.D., and Peter D. Rogers, Ph.D. Oakland: New Harbinger Publications, 2000.
- *Don't Sweat the Small Stuff . . . And It's All Small Stuff: Simple Ways to Keep the Little Things from Taking Over Your Life* by Richard Carlson, Ph.D. New York: Hyperion, 1997.
- *Living a Beautiful Life* by Alexandra Stoddard. New York: Quill/HarperResource, 2001.
- *The Pathways to Peace Anger Management Workbook*, by William Fleeman. Alameda, Calif.: Hunter House, 2003.
- *When Anger Hurts: Quieting the Storm Within* by Matthew McKay, Ph.D., Peter D. Rogers, Ph.D., and Judith McKay, R.N. Oakland: New Harbinger Publications, 2003.

Grief and Loss
- *25 Things to Do When Grandpa Passes Away, Mom and Dad Get Divorced, or the Dog Dies: Activities to Help Children Suffering Loss or Change* by Laurie A. Kanyer, M.A., Seattle: Parenting Press, 2004.
- *Helping Children Cope with Separation and Loss*, rev. ed., by Claudia Jewett Jaratt. Boston: Harvard Common Press, 1994.

Attachment/Trauma
- *Becoming Attached: First Relationships and How They Shape Our Capacity to Love* by Robert Karen, Ph.D. New York: Oxford University Press, 1998.

- *Building the Bonds of Attachment: Awakening Love in Deeply Troubled Children,* 2nd ed., by Daniel A. Hughes. Lanham, Md.: Jason Aronson, 2006.
- *Facilitating Developmental Attachment: The Road to Emotional Recovery and Behavioral Change in Foster and Adopted Children* by Daniel A. Hughes. Lanham, Md.: Jason Aronson, 2000.
- *Theraplay: Helping Parents and Children Build Better Relationships Through Attachment-Based Play,* 2nd ed., by Anne M. Jernberg and Phyllis B. Booth. San Francisco: Jossey-Bass, 1998.

Children's Books
- *Alexander and the Terrible, Horrible, No-Good, Very Bad Day,* rev. ed., by Judith Viorst. New York: Aladdin, 1987.
- *Andrew's Angry Words* by Dorothea Lachner. New York: North-South Books, 1995.
- *How to Take the Grrrr Out of Anger* by Elizabeth Verdick and Marjorie Lisovkis. Minneapolis, Minn.: Free Spirit Publishing, 2003.
- *I Don't Want to Talk About It* by Jeanie Franz Ransom. Washington, D.C.: Magination Press, 2000. (About divorce)
- *I'm Frustrated* by Elizabeth Crary. Seattle: Parenting Press, 1992.
- *I'm Furious* by Elizabeth Crary. Seattle: Parenting Press, 1993.
- *I'm Mad* by Elizabeth Crary. Seattle: Parenting Press, 1992.
- *The Way I Feel* by Janan Cain. Seattle: Parenting Press, 2000.
- *What About Me? 12 Ways to Get Your Parents' Attention (Without Hitting Your Sister)* by Eileen Kennedy-Moore. Seattle: Parenting Press, 2005.
- *When Sophie Gets Angry—Really, Really Angry* by Molly Bang. New York: The Blue Sky Press (Scholastic imprint), 1999.

Index

Entries in quotation marks are exercises or charts.

A

active listening, how-to, 36-41

aggression: physical, 52-6; verbal, 32-3

anger: cover-up for other emotions, 11; expression in adults, 90-3; protective value of, 9; questionaire, 132-3; signs of child's immediate need for help, 105

anger-isms, 93

angry parents. *See* parents, angry

ask for help, 47

attachment, importance of, 20-1; 120

attention seeking behavior, 56, 59

B

"Basic Feelings Vocabulary," 32

basic needs, unfilled as source of anger, 17

breathing, deep, 43

C

calming techniques: ask for help, 47; count to ten, 44; expend angry energy safely, 47-8; positive outcome visualization, 46; positive self-talk, 44-5; relaxation visualization, 45; take deep breaths, 43; time-out, 48-9; verbalize feelings, 46

"Characteristics of a Rejuvenating Friendship," 100

coach, parent as, 27, 64-6

coaching, for dealing with feelings, 43-7

"Common Mistakes in Handling Grief," 81

conflict management, 69-73; 124-7

consistency in using skills, 102-3

consultant, parent as, 67-8

co-parenting, 96-8; 130-1

count to ten, 44

cursing, 33

D

decisions, making good decisions while angry, 48

development, effect on child's anger, 13, 19; 110-19

divorce, acute source of

anger, 83-4

E
emotional problems need-
   ing immediate help, 105
empathy, showing, 29-30
"Exercise: Evaluating
   Parental Anger," 92
"Exercise: How Skillfully
   Do You Manage Anger?"
   13
"Exercise: Prioritizing
   Parental Values," 89

F
faces, making, to teach
   feelings vocabulary, 31
family-centered sources of
   anger, 21
feelings vocabulary: basic,
   32; building, 30-3; lack
   of as factor in anger, 12
"Five Laws of
   Co-Parenting," 97-8
"Five Steps to Conflict
   Management," 73
frustration tolerance, lack
   of as factor in anger, 12

G
good decisions, making
   while angry, 48
grief: expression of, 82-3;
   mishandling of, 81; stages of, 82
"Guidelines for Choosing a
   Professional Therapist,"
106-7

H
health: of child, 19; of parent, 16, 21, 88, 104-5
hitting. *See* aggression
holding an angry child
   safely, 53, 55-6
"How Brain Wiring
   Impacts Anger," 18

I
"I feel . . ." (faces illustra-
   tion), 31
"I-Message" how-to, 34
I-messages, modeling and
   teaching, 33-6
impulse control, lack of as
   factor in anger, 12
"Influences on a Child's
   Anger," 17

L
life circumstances: death,
   divorce, foster care,
   moving, 75, 80-3, 84-5
life experience, lack of as
   factor in anger, 11, 20
limit setting, 74-9
logical consequences, 80,
   93
loss of control in child,
   55-6

M
making good decisions
   while angry, 48
manipulation, 59

media, influence on children, 24-5

modeling appropriate behavior, importance of, 27, 32, 48, 49, 88

N

natural consequences, 79-80, 93

nonnegotiable limits, 74-9

"Normal Versus Problem Anger," 14

P

parent as conflict manager, 70-2

parent as judge, 69-70

"Parent as Judge/Parent as Conflict Manager," 70

parents, angry: behavior, 88; conflicting values in, 88-9; co-parenting laws for, 97-8; expressing feelings, 90-2; realistic expectations and, 90; reasons for, 88; preventing through self-care, 94-6; social support for, 99-100

parents, healthy: as partners, 96-8; awareness of own feelings, 78-9; benefits of, 23-4; managing own anger, 87-8; self-care, 94-5

patience, requirement for helping angry kids, 42, 72-3, —for changing oneself, 93, 102-3

peers: anger compared to, 15; impact of, 25

positive self-talk, 44

primary feelings, 10-1, 28-9, 30

"Primary Versus Secondary Feelings," 10

problem-solving skills: coach, 64, 65-6; consultant, 67-8; lack of as factor in anger, 12; nurturer, 63; teaching individual skills, 61-8; teaching social skills, 69-73

public, angry behavior in, 57-8

R

realistic expectations, 90

reflecting feelings, 36-41

reinforcement system, 128-9

relaxation visualization, 45

"Replacing Common Parental Anger-isms," 93

rescuing, 74-9

role of parent, 14; 110-19

S

safe ways to expend angry energy, 47-8

secondary feelings, 10-1

self-care for adults, 94-5

"Self-Care Ideas," 94-5
self-injury, 59-60
signs of anger in children,
6, 14, 105
social environment as factor in anger, 25
social support for parents,
99
sources of anger: brain
wiring, 18-9; child-cen-
tered, 17-21; family-cen-
tered, 21-4; environ-
ment-based, 24-5; life
circumstances, 80-6
"Steps to Parent-Guided
Individual Problem
Solving," 62
stress in families, 104-5
swearing, 33

T

tantrums, dealing with,
54, 57-8, 59
teaching skills: for dealing with feelings, 43-7;
importance of, 27

television, influence on
children, 24-5
temperament, affect on
anger, 19
therapists/therapy, how to
choose, 106-7; when to
look for, 103-7; where to
find, 106-7
time-out: 33, how-to, 49;
parent modeling, 49-50;
questions about, 121-3;
taking child to, 52-5;
teaching child to use,
51-2
"Time-Out Basics," 49
trauma in child's life, 21-3,
80-6, 104

V

values, family: impact on
anger, 88-90; prioritiz-
ing, 88-90
verbal aggression, 33
verbalize feelings, 46

Your Notes

More helpful resources for parents and caregivers

Is This a Phase? Child Development & Parent Strategies, Birth to 6 Years describes children's typical development in the fast-changing early years of a child's life. The author answers parents' most common concerns, such as: Is my baby crying too much? my 2-year-old won't share, my 3-year-old is still in diapers, my 4-year-old says mean things and lies, my 5-year-old isn't ready for kindergarten, and much more. Many charts provide quick information for busy adults. Author **Helen F. Neville,** illustrator Jenny Williams. ISBN 978-1-884734-63-2. **$22.95** paperback

Unplugging Power Struggles: Resolving Emotional Battles with Your Kids, Ages 2 to 10 helps parents prevent or resolve battles over who can do what, when. Learn *when* and *how* to hold on to power, to allow the child to assume it (gradually), or to drop back or out of the struggle. Author **Jan Faull.** ISBN 978-1-884734-42-7. **$13.95** paperback

Dealing with Disappointment: Helping Kids Cope When Things Don't Go Their Way acknowledges the fact that things don't always go our way, whether we're 5, or 15, or all grown up. It offers tools and techniques parents can use to teach children to cope, whether through a toddler tantrum or a middle-school meltdown. Author **Elizabeth Crary.** ISBN 978-1-884734-75-5. **$13.95** paperback

Self-Calming Cards (Tarjetas para calmarse) is a deck of 36 cards with the instruction sheet in English and Spanish. These 24 self-calming tools and 12

activity cards help children (and adults) learn self-calming strategies while having lots of fun. Children who have self-calming skills recover from emotional upset more quickly, get along better with everyone, switch from one activity to another more easily, and think more clearly and calmly in emergencies. Author **Elizabeth Crary** and illustrator **Mits Katayama.** For ages 2-12 years. **$12.95** deck

What About Me? 12 Ways to Get Your Parents' Attention (Without Hitting Your Sister) offers 12 positive, practical, and possible ways for a small child to get attention from grown-ups when he or she is feeling left out. Helpful for a child with a new sibling or for any child with several siblings. Author **Eileen Kennedy-Moore** and illustrator **Mits Katayama.** For ages 3-8 years. ISBN 978-1-884734-86-1. **$14.94** hardcover

The Way I Feel is a child's feelings word book. Children need to be able to name their feelings even more than they need to be able to name animals, toys, and colors. This book offers vivid illustrations that the youngest child can understand and realistic verses defining the feeling. Two-year-olds are known to have told their parents they are "frustrated" or "proud" after having this book read to them as often as they like. Author and illustrator **Janan Cain.** For ages 2-8 years. ISBN 978-1-884734-71-7. **$16.95** hardcover

Ask for these books at your favorite bookstore, call 1-800-992-6657, or visit us on the Internet at www.ParentingPress.com. Visa and MasterCard accepted. A complete catalogue is on our web site. Prices subject to change without notice. In Canada, call Raincoast Books Express, 1-800-663-5714.